Penguin Books
An Open Book

Monica Dickens, great-granddaughter of Charles Dickens, has written over thirty novels, autobiographical books and children's books, and her works are beginning to be adapted for television and film. Her first book, *One Pair of Hands*, which arose out of her experiences as a cook-general – the only work for which her upper-class education had fitted her – made her a best seller at twenty-two, and is still in great demand.

Although her books arise out of the varied experiences of her life, she has not taken jobs in order to write about them: working in an aircraft factory and a hospital was her war work, not research. When she joined the Samaritans, it was the work of befriending distressed fellow human beings which she found compelling, although her novel *The Listeners* came from that experience.

She set up the first American branch of the Samaritans in Boston, Massachusetts, and lives nearby on Cape Cod with her husband Commander Roy Stratton, retired from the U.S. Navy, and her horses, cats and dogs. She has two daughters.

Monica Dickens

An Open Book

Penguin Books

Penguin Books Ltd, Harmondsworth,
Middlesex, England
Penguin Books, 625 Madison Avenue,
New York, New York 10022, U.S.A.
Penguin Books Australia Ltd, Ringwood,
Victoria, Australia
Penguin Books Canada Ltd, 2801 John Street,
Markham, Ontario, Canada L3R 1B4
Penguin Books (N.Z.) Ltd, 182–190 Wairau Road,
Auckland 10, New Zealand

First published by William Heinemann Ltd 1978
Published in Penguin Books 1980
Copyright © Monica Dickens, 1978
All rights reserved.

Made and printed in Great Britain by
Hazell Watson & Viney Ltd,
Aylesbury, Bucks
Set in Linotype Times

Contents

Acknowledgements

The majority of the photographs which appear in this book are from the author's, and her family's, own private collections. The author is however indebted to *Woman's Own*, Yorkshire Television, Thames Television, and George Konig for their assistance with certain of the photographs.

A small number of illustrations are of unknown provenance and are believed not to be the subject of claimed copyright. If copyright is claimed in any of them the publishers will be pleased to correspond with the claimant and to make any arrangements which may prove to be appropriate.

Illustrations

An Open Book

1

This is not the whole story of a life. It is an attempt to re-capture some of those elements of it which are the origins of books that I have written.

So childhood must be looked at, not only because I have written children's books, self-indulgently for the child still within, but because it is both the soil and the roots of what grows later.

No one can remember being born. The machinery of memory seems to start recording only with the first breath, and the recovery system much later. Although there is evidence that the act of dying may involve a second journey through a dark tunnel into light, there is no memory of that first adventure. It is difficult even to imagine the process of being born – and to one's own *mother*? Impossible. We have to take it on faith, since they tell us that it was so. Imagination starts with the brass bed in the front room of a late Georgian house in West London, with raffish Portobello Road at the side, and respectable Chepstow Villas at the front, where an early milk horse shuffles from house to house through the yellow dust of fallen plane-tree blossoms. My mother, with two live children and the exhaustion of a miscarriage and twin babies who died, is glad to have got it over, with any luck for the last time, since she is nearly forty.

A photograph shows her with her thin dark hair puffed out at the sides, in bed with the baby, as she was allowed to be for two luxurious weeks, with Nurse Henly-Smith back in office for the fourth time.

In the security of being in bed with Mother, the baby looks smug, as if already aware of the extra confidence of being the youngest. *It stops with me. That's all they need now.* To be the eldest, and find more babies following, must give you the uneasy suspicion that you are not enough.

Active memory starts soon after two, with a maid screaming, 'The Zepps are coming!' and flinging an apron over her head. When the police blew whistles in the streets on moonlit nights, we slept under a mattress folded backwards to make a cave against the anti-aircraft shell splinters that were more dangerous than German Zeppelins.

My mother was a paisley coat with a band of fur round the bottom at eye level, on which I clung and hung and buried my yawns while she chatted interminably on street corners.

My father was a front door banging and a shout of, 'Where's my baby?', and a pyramid of soft sawdust growing on the dining room carpet where I sat while he cut out jigsaw puzzles on his treadle fretsaw.

My brother, nine years older than me, was a god, hardly known, away at school and then at the Naval College, coming home in cadet's uniform to do things we were not allowed to do, like drinking wine and putting his feet up on the sofa. When he was there, I waited for his notice, and watched his moods to grab my chance of making him laugh.

My sister Doris, called Doady because of David Copperfield, was a year and a half above me. She used to lecture me on how to grow up, but I always felt it should be the other way round. She cried from sentiment, not from rage, and was more easily hurt. She forgot her glasses and could not see at plays and pantomimes. She always needed to go to the lavatory. Once when we were late for the circus, they had to pull up the floorboard of a cab for her in Kensington High Street.

When she was five, my mother taught her to read from a red cloth book called *Reading Without Tears*, and I sat under the table and absorbed it unconsciously from floor level. With no will or skill involved, I could read at three and a half. As I got older, I found that I could win at paper games and children's party contests, and that if I did not win, I did not enjoy playing. I was 'that clever little Moaneeca' to great aunts with names like

Medusa and Octavie. Not to aunts, whose children were competing, but Dusa and VV and Great Uncle Rhubarb patted my square stubborn head and wished I would not frown so much.

In memory, everybody of the Dusa and VV generation on both sides of the family had a strong foreign accent and eccentric gestures, played music, acted, painted, invented gadgets and manufactured a lot of saliva. My grandfather, Henry Fielding Dickens, who was Charles Dickens's eighth child and sixth son, married Marie Roche, whose father was French and whose grandfather was the German musician Ignaz Moscheles, pupil of Beethoven. When Beethoven was ill and destitute and starving to death, Ignaz, with two people called 'Sir Smart and Herr Stumpff' brought succour, but too late.

My mother's father, Herman Runge, came from Bremen. He went to Cuba to start a prosperous business in sugar, which was later absorbed into the British firm of Tate and Lyle. He married a German girl, Emma Philippi, and they settled in Dulwich with their family, who were called Emma, Fanny, Daisy, Gerty and Julius.

During the spy paranoia of the First War, Herman changed the pronunciation of his name from the German Roong-er to Runge, rhyming with sponge. Although he was producing for England tons of sugar and jam, including the '*Plum* and ap-pul, *ap*-pul and plum' the Tommies sang about, he had been suspected of being an enemy agent, with a name like that, and money too. When he built a tennis court at his country house in Somerset, miles away from any military area, local people said it was a gun emplacement.

In the Second War, I knew a dentist in Aberdovey, North Wales, who was inventing an electric toothbrush, and the people in that flint and slate hill town heard the buzzing through an open window and said that he was sending code messages to the Nazis.

My father's name was Henry Charles Dickens. Everybody called him Hal. My mother had been christened only Fanny. When I was a child, I must have called them Mummy and Daddy, but it seemed natural to start calling them Henry and

Fanny when I was still quite young. It is only now that I am surprised at how progressive they were about it.

Fanny's parents lived in a spacious flat as big as a house at the north-east corner of Berkeley Square. Almost every Sunday, we walked across Kensington Gardens and Hyde Park and through Grosvenor Square to a rather formal tea, with damp cucumber sandwiches and *Sachertorte*. The walks of childhood were endless. It was only when it rained that we went by Tube, or on the open top of a bus, with Henry's brolly up and the tarpaulin apron buttoned across our waists.

Every spring and summer holidays, we went to Chilworthy, the grandparents' Elizabethan house near Chard, in Somerset.

The Runge family was just as clannish and gregarious as the Dickenses. There never seemed to be less than twenty or thirty people at Chilworthy, not counting the servants. Emma, Fanny, Daisy, Gerty and Julius were almost always there, with Frank, Hal, Percy, Archie and Norah and their children, plus various friends and in-laws.

Chilworthy, of course, was much smaller than I remembered when I first revisited it as a grown-up. The endless drive was less than a hundred yards. The house was a comfortable small manor house, not a palace. To a child, it was a whole vast world of unending discoveries, inhabited by many different societies and cultures.

Fanny's father we hardly ever spoke to. He stumped about dressed as an English squire in a tweed Norfolk jacket, cord breeches and buttoned leather gaiters over square-toed boots. Sometimes he carried a riding whip, though I never saw him ride, sometimes a gun, sometimes a cane to tap the gaiters with. He had a sustained German accent, stiff grey hair and cornflower blue eyes, over which I watched, as he grew older, a mysterious brush wash to dim and moisten.

He was polite and generous to all his guests and tolerant of his welter of freeloading grandchildren, but rather remote and frightening to us. I see him standing squarely on the back drive talking earnestly to a gardener, while I hovered unnoticed to catch a threat about pruning the neglected hedge where my cousin Phoebe and I put out crumbs and lavender cachous for the fairies. My dog, with the careless arrogance of a London terrier, lifted its leg against Herman Runge's leather gaiter. He went on talking, while Spot scratched up a little hind leg gravel and wandered off. I grabbed him and hid him for the rest of the day in a shed behind the pump house, in case he was shot by Grandpa, or one of the temporary sportsmen who walked with guns in the crook of an elbow over the listening rabbit colonies under the park.

Fanny's mother was so little known to me that I had to ask what her name was when I was writing this book. She was as remote as Grandpa, but less intimidating. She was a bundle of clothes without legs, blacks and greys and mauves, with a high lace collar held up by stays that looked as if it was pinned into her neck.

She had, or was said to have, a weakness of the heart, and some doctor had condemned her, while still quite young, to the life of an invalid. At forty, she put on a lace cap, sign of submission to middle age, and spent her days in bed, or propped in a pillowed chair. She sat sometimes in her drawing room, with her feet on a stool tapestried for her by Henry's mother, and the lovely lawns and parkland rolling away before her captive eyes; but she never came to the dining room for meals, or sat around the fire in the big central hall where family and guests drank whisky and sherry and ate gigantic teas with six kinds of cake two hours before dinner time.

On warm days in the garden, where wasps drowned muzzily in traps of stale beer, she sat in a hooded wicker chair like a sentry box that shielded her from noise and sun. At raspberry time or when the peaches from the kitchen garden were ripe, she occasionally joined the tea party in the summer house, to which maids with blowing aprons brought out the fruit and silver jugs of yellow Jersey cream from the farm.

We children usually spoke to her only once a day. One by one before bedtime, we went in to the warm scented room where Granny lay in a downy bed not shared by Grandpa for years, spooning a soft boiled egg with chopped toast and sherry out of a Meissen cup.

Sometimes you got a heady taste of the egg. Every evening,

you got a square of Nestlé's chocolate wrapped in silver paper. Granny did not ask us how we were or what we had been doing, and we did not stay long enough to tell, but you had the impression of approval, and of a rather wistful need for these pyjamaed visits. Even when she was too ill to count her grandchildren, you would not have dreamed of missing your turn, even after there was no more chocolate.

The other grown-ups at Chilworthy, including our parents, were almost as remote to us as our grandparents. They lived on a level above us, an upper atmosphere, touchable but unknown. They must have been having fights and love affairs and intrigues and nerve storms and great jokes, but in memory they existed only as a cast of extras, mostly off stage, in the dramas played out by the children. Once a week, we took turns to have lunch in the dining room, an elegant room with a long table surrounded by voices, and two parlourmaids standing by the sideboard where Archie or Hal carved sides of beef or four roast chickens at a time. Dining room lunch meant putting on a dress instead of the boy's shirt and flannel shorts and snake-buckle belt we wore at Chilworthy, before clothes like that were made for girls. The torture of shyness was mitigated by the roast beef and the gooseberry fool and the salty black-currant ice cream which was made by the kitchen maid endlessly churning a handle in the cool stone-flagged scullery.

The children's meals were in the nursery, where we lived in the nannies' half-world, between the grown-ups and the servants, with Nanny Gathergood, Miss Roser, Mary Mobsby, and other dear good women in long brown skirts. Our bedrooms were at the top of one wing of the house, small white-painted rooms where the very young had hot milk and petits beurres for supper, and the older ones visited from room to room by way of the roofs and twisted chimney stacks after we had been shut away for the night.

In another wing were the maids' bedrooms, stuffy under the roof, not painted white. Downstairs beyond the green baize swing door were the tiled kitchen and the sculleries and pantries and larders, a stone cell where sadly-plumed game birds hung

16

in pairs and upside-down hares had buckets on their noses to catch the blood, and the butler's pantry where the early morning tea trays were set out the night before.

A child might go to the kitchen or pantry with a message from one of the nannies who did not dare to ring a bell, but never into the servants' hall or sitting room. You might chat to a maid in a print dress brushing the wide staircase on hands and knees, or wink your left eye at a parlourmaid as she tilted the meat so you could get more gravy, but beyond the green baize their lives were as inviolate as the world of the grown-ups or the nannies or the children.

The housekeeper, who had her own rooms at the top of a little stair by Gerty's room, and Annie Bavin, who was Granny's lady's maid with her own bedroom to sew in, were on still another level. We visited Annie for bandages and ointment and empty cotton reels to braid wool, but never the housekeeper, and they only visited the nursery by invitation for tea or morning cocoa. Annie, with pins in her alpaca dress, had her meals in the servants' hall, but the housekeeper had trays carried to her room by a young housemaid with a flushed face and burred Ilminster voice. There was a chauffeur called Hawley, who drove the Lancia tourer and the upright Renault with the same care and finesse with which he had once driven his carriage bays, a groom for the few remaining riding horses, many gardeners and a man who ran the generator in a throbbing shed at the back of the laurel shrubbery.

The world of the children was as little known to the grown-ups as theirs was to us. There were fiercely bonded friendships, loosening in the distances of different schools in term time and re-forming with someone else next holidays. There were gang wars, pogroms against the nurses, love affairs, hero worship, torture sessions, hauntings, obsessive cults, and displays of long distance urination by the boys.

My sister Doady, gangling and troubled by sin and endlessly creative, wrote dramas with titles like *The Lost Prince* and *Love's Golden Ending*, which we acted in the playhouse with the sandpit, and forced the grown-ups to watch. Like a Hollywood script writer, Doady had to rewrite her dialogue continually to suit the cast. Phoebe, who was the naughtiest of all the cousins, would only play a virtuous character. Ian had to be the hero. Nancy would act but not speak, and I would only play comic charwomen.

Beyond the playhouse and the ha-ha wall which bounded the cricket lawn, mowed by a donkey wearing leather boots, the thistles and long grass of the park sloped down to a pond which had been dredged out for swimming. Water snakes slithered in and out of the pilings that shored up its muddy banks, and the diving board had a pole at the end of it, so that cousin George could balance there after he had taken off his wooden leg.

The bathing huts smelled of rotting wet wood, the water garden smelled astringently of primulas. The whole house smelled of lavender and wood smoke. The gong under the stairs divided the long days by meal times.

Chilworthy, still very clear in the memory of all the senses, appeared in my first two books, and seems to have crept in through cracks in many of the others. I still feel sad at the smell of the first raspberries.

When her father and mother died and the Somerset house was sold, Fanny, anticipating the shock of loss, was already negotiating to buy a cottage in Oxfordshire with a young friend who would keep ponies for us. We still saw the cousins at Christmas and family occasions, and on the clan holidays in Belgium, but with the end of Chilworthy there had been an immediate fading of the intensity of loves and hates that had thrived in that privileged paradise at the end of the Taunton train from Paddington and the branch line to Chard.

2

Knowing now how few people enjoy that kind of security and knowledge of love, I marvel at a childhood that I once took for granted.

Apart from the bourgeois entrenchment of the large Runge and Dickens families, there was the strengthening reassurance of parents who thought you were all right, and frequently told you so. Fanny was too small and bony for bosomy cuddling and knee-sitting, but if you hurled yourself into her arms, she would pat you on the back, after she recovered her balance, and hum at you. She never sat still for very long, but Henry was in one place for hours, reading or making lists or cutting out jigsaws from posters pasted onto plywood, his lap always available as an extra piece of warm furniture.

Of course I thought them dreadfully old-fashioned and restrictive and obtuse and embarrassing. That in itself was a stable thing, since they did not change to suit my opinions. I did not really want them to change, and they did not even try to change me. If I was scowling and sullen, it was not, 'Don't behave like that.' It was, 'She's scowling and sullen.'

One of the things that helped to make the relationship satisfactory was that we did not see each other all the time. I would not for anything have missed bringing up my own small children, but I do see that there was something to be said for the old nanny system, of which my generation was the last to benefit.

This was the last respite of family innocence before the revelations of the early Thirties shook parents with the new ideas of child psychology. Children must no longer be seen as being 'naughty' or 'good' at will. There were deep and disturbing reasons why they did what they did. More disturbing still: if bringing up children was really such a ticklish intellectual exercise, requiring great sensitivity and imagination on the part of parents, how had it always been handled so well by darling old Nanny with her hairy mole, who had been in the family for three generations and smelled of bread and butter?

With us in the unenlightened Twenties, it was Nanny Gathergood who changed the nappies, washed the clothes, untangled the hair, tutted and scolded and picked up hurled food, got us up in time for school and listened patiently, sewing, to childhood sagas. One was not always hearing, 'Don't' from one's mother, nor the news that we were driving her into an early grave.

What exhausted mother has not been guilty of crying, 'One day I'm going to walk right out of this house and never come back!'

I said it once too often, and when I stepped out unseen to borrow a bread tin next door, my child had hysterics, because she thought I had done it.

Nanny never said that she would die, or go insane, or leave us. If she had, we would not have believed it .

She was the sun and moon of our days and nights. It was to her that we went first in trouble.

She came to us just before I was born, a nineteen-year-old Norfolk girl, charmingly called Ethel May Gathergood. And she did gather good out of her warm, unselfish heart and heap it on our family. She stayed with us for thirty years, going on to take care of my brother's baby after I was grown up.

She was a staple of childhood, nourishing and safe, existing, we thought, only for us. It was only years later, after she had gone back to King's Lynn to take care of her elderly mother in the little brick cottage by the railway station, that I was able to see her as a woman, and not just as my Nanny Gathergood. I worried about her having given up all the productive years of her life to us. What had we done to her? How selfish we had been in assuming that she was happy, making her life round our family. If there was some good in the nanny system, was it only for those on the receiving end?

She wrote to me recently from the brick cottage by the railway station, where her mother used to play hymns for us when we visited cosily as children.

'Being nineteen, I never expected to stay with you thirty years, but the war came and I was very happy and felt it was my war job, as your mother had a job. Your mother was kindness itself, and there was a very happy atmosphere, and I felt I grew up with you.

'When I left, it took a time to settle down after such a wrench. It was a wonderful life. I have never regretted it, and it leaves very happy memories.'

So it does to me, Ethel May Gathergood. So it does to me.

Fanny, a woman ahead of her time, was with us much more than most other mothers were. She devised treats, and spent all her time with us when we went abroad. She read to us and played paper games and made a boat with the dining room table upside down, and a mountain with a mattress and a tea tray on the stairs. She was pleasure and stimulation, but Nanny Gathergood was our bread and butter.

Henry was also ahead of his time in his interest in small children. Every morning while he was shaving with one of seven cut-throat razors marked for different days of the week, we had to go into his dressing room for Catechism or French lessons. Beyond the macabre interest of seeing him nick himself and stem the sudsy blood with Bronco toilet paper, we hated it. There were always tears and violence. In winter, the rungs of the cane-seated chair in front of the popping gas fire were scarred by angry heels. In summer, patches of the leather top of the old table by the window were picked as clean as a prairie dog's carcase. Henry gave us twopence if we were good. Since we were never good, he gave us the twopence anyway.

In the evening when he came home from what was known as going to the Bar, he would throw open the front door and fling it shut with a crash that shook the square house, whistle hopefully and shout, 'Where's my baby?'

Before I learned to sulk and play hard to get, My Baby was

coming down the stairs one step at a time, later sliding down the banister, a perfect smooth rail with no knob at the end, so that you could land halfway across the hall.

I came down again in a dressing gown to the dining room after dinner for nuts and crystallized plums, and then Henry would come upstairs and read to me in bed. He loved to read aloud, and did not mind if you fell asleep. When we went through the childhood illnesses, which were more numerous and lengthy in those days, and required long spells in bed in a dim light, he read Dickens to us. Reading *Great Expectations* for myself years later, I realized how much I had missed as I drifted in and out of consciousness.

He had been reading to his wife ever since they were engaged. In his desk among the many lists of symphonies he had heard on the wireless, places he had travelled to, dinner parties, records of his blood pressure, dates of *The Times* crossword puzzles he had not finished, there was a long paper called 'Books I Have Read to Fan'. My brother claimed to have found a shorter list called 'Books I Have Not Read to Fan'.

In the last illness of her old age, he would stump up the stairs every evening with Pett Ridge or Jane Austen or Jerome K. Jerome, and read to her for hours, even when she hardly knew that he was there. After she died, he was found once or twice with his foot on the bottom stair and a book in his hand.

'Where are you going, darling?'

'Just going up to read to your mother.'

Another routine of childhood was the weekly visit to Henry's mother in Chelsea, with tussore dresses and white socks laid out the night before, and patent leather shoes cleaned with milk. We groaned when Nanny put out the clothes and came at us with strips of rag to curl our hair, but it was at least a confirmation of the continuation of life, like the early morning tea trays set out in the butler's pantry at Chilworthy, and laying the breakfast table at night, to ensure that morning will come. Doady and I started to do that when I stayed with her in wartime. I still rinse out the coffee mugs at midnight and put them upside down on the chopping board by the stove, as a talisman of survival.

When Nanny put the clothes on me, I fretted and fussed, hoping to be hit with the bristles of the hairbrush, which might bring out a rash I could claim as a disease. Nanny disliked going to 8 Mulberry Walk as much as we did. My grandmother was a passionate and devoted Frenchwoman, an argumentative tribal chief, who used to shout at her maids, 'Fool!' and '*Grande bête!*'

Nanny was afraid of her, as Fanny had been when she was engaged, and even when she was first married. When Henry fell in love with the trimly skating figure at St Moritz, his parents were indulgent of a holiday romance with the small dark girl whose parents were at least staying at the right hotel. But marriage . . .

Herman Runge had more money than they did, but it was unfortunate that he was 'in trade'. Unaware of disapproval, Herman was busy with his own reservations, since Henry was not only a struggling young barrister, but had been brought up a Roman Catholic.

When Henry and Fanny were at last allowed to marry, after a four year engagement, they had to go to supper at Mulberry Walk every Sunday night. Henry's brothers and sisters, Enid, Gerald, Elaine, Olive, Pip and Ceddy, were noisy and clannish and opinionated. His father, a canny, humorous small man with a long legal upper lip and Charles Dickens's folded eyelids, seldom spoke to anyone. He was known as The Guvnor. His wife, The Mater, shouted friendly abuse at the servants and was bossy with Fanny, which made her sweat and tremble, although she always came home with a cake or half a chicken, which they were too poor to refuse. As time went on and Fanny had children of her own, she learned to love her mother-in-law and to boss her back, which worked much better than sweating and trembling.

Doady and I were not afraid of our grandmother. We liked her pride in us, but were embarrassed by her French matriarchal attention and energetic projects. Acting our own feeble plays in the sand house at Chilworthy was one thing. Stumbling and mumbling to order through comic rhymed sketches in French was another.

Following the theatrical obsession of Charles Dickens, there were always plays being performed by someone somewhere in that family. They had known great actors like Henry Irving and Fechter, but that did not discourage them from constant amateur dramatics.

At Christmas, when there were never less than fifty people in the billiard room at the top of 8 Mulberry Walk, the Guvnor did imitations of his father giving his famous 'Readings', which were recitations by heart from his own books. He did Sairey Gamp and the murder of Nancy from *Oliver Twist* – 'Bill, Bill, for dear God's sake, for your own, for mine, stop before you spill my blood!' – which had raised Charles Dickens's pulse and blood pressure dangerously when he performed it in America shortly before his death. His eldest son Charley, who was with him on the American tour, is said to have been told by the doctor, 'If you see your father falter in the least, you must run and catch him and bring him off to me, or by heaven, he'll die before them all.'

Henry Fielding Dickens wore a geranium and leaned his elbow on the same velvet-covered reading stand. He had listened to his father many times, and the older ones said he was amazingly like Charles Dickens. To celebrate his eightieth birthday, he went the whole way through *A Christmas Carol* without a hitch, his teeth loosening at the melodramatic bits: 'I know him – Marley's ghosht!'

To a child, having a famous ancestor did not seem important. The grown-ups talked a lot about Dickens and took us to be photographed putting flowers on his gravestone in the floor of Westminster Abbey, but it meant nothing much in our ego-centric lives. It is hard now to accept that my grandfather had known Charles Dickens intimately, and I never thought of asking him about it.

Fanny, even though her family was 'in trade', was just as

creative as the Dickenses. She had been writing dramas and
romances and poems all her life. All family anniversaries and
startling occasions like Herman Runge winning a skating medal
– '. . . you tightened every nerve, to get the proper perfect
curve' – were celebrated by her in the special brand of doggerel
verse that flowed out of her like water.

> 'A year ago today you were Miss Runge.
> At half past 2 you took the fatal plunge,
> That seemed across our lives to draw a sponge
> Which left them blank.'

> 'Hail little stranger fat and fair,
> At three and twenty Carlyle Square.'

> 'A year ago today you were Miss Dickens.
> My thoughts fly back a year, and linger there.
> I seem to see a crowd that swells and thickens
> And fills the hall and oozes up the stair.'

> 'I cannot well describe my feeling
> When *Times* in hand and egg begun,
> I saw that Mrs Dickens, Ealing
> Had chosen to produce a son.'

As the family children increased, she wrote the book and
lyrics for several excellent musicals, which she and her ambitious sisters-in-law produced in real theatres, ostensibly for
charity, but really because they wanted to produce plays.

To the music of Great-Aunt Nina, granddaughter of Ignaz
Moscheles, we sang:

> 'We'll bring back a bit of the rainbow.
> We'll fold it and pack it up tight,
> For Mother to wear in her beautiful hair
> When she goes to big parties at night.'

In the Nanny era of hot milk and petits beurres, if your
mother went out every night in her georgette and swansdown,
you could see it as romantic, not depriving.

For one of her heroes, in the style she originated as a swoony girl in Dulwich, Fanny wrote:

> 'Ah, strange indeed were I dismay'd,
> E'en at the prospect laid before me.
> I lose my life, or win a wife
> Of beauty rare, who will no doubt adore me.'

Shades of her marriage in that last line, which reeks placidly of Dickens male egotism.

The mother of Henry, Enid, Gerald, Elaine (known as Bobby), Olive, Pip and Ceddy, known as Mumsey when she was not The Mater, brought up her sons as the salt of the earth.

'So we were,' Henry grunted, when I said this to him.

The most beloved was the youngest one, Ceddy, who was killed, with 101,872 other Allied soldiers, at the Battle of the Somme in 1916. She kept a full size replica of the cross at the head of his grave in a frame in her bedroom, with a *prie-dieu* in front of it.

After the war, when they told her that he had been buried on the spot where he fell near Ginchy, she bought the land and put up the white cross and made a little garden with a hedge round it. Every year she took the Channel boat to Boulogne and went by train to visit the cemetery garden in the middle of a field, and pay the man who took care of it.

Some time after she died in 1940, the War Graves Commission asked the family if they could move the remains to a military cemetery. When the grave was dug up, there was nothing there. There never had been. No bones. Nothing. When Ceddy was blown up, there had been nothing left of him to bury. The old lady had been making her healing pilgrimages to a patch of empty earth.

When I was old enough to follow Doady to school, Nanny Gathergood walked us across Ladbroke Square and down Holland Park Avenue to Norland Place School, and was waiting among the crowd of other nannies with prams and terriers on leads to walk us home again.

We always chose the same streets, because I was learning the life in the basements of the terrace houses, and had to keep up with what was going on. The remnants of breakfast. Preparations for tea. A maid fitting on her cap at a small mirror behind a cupboard door. Children playing cards. Two people arguing, with pointing fingers. A man in braces with an eaten-away nose who had once come to the window full face, just as we passed ('Don't look, Monica').

It was the first stirring of the passion for glimpsed lives, the beginning of the struggle, still not yet won, to understand why the scene looks so seductive when you are outside it, yet if you were inside, the outsider walking by would hold the key to romance and adventure.

Norland Place was a splendid small school which cost five pounds a term and not only taught, but taught you how to learn.

Although term reports indicate I was a nuisance, and speak politely about needing 'to exercise more self control and consideration for others,' what I wrote for the school's centenary in 1976, is what I think I did feel at the time:

'. . . the security of that between-wars world where Norland Place, in some inspired and understanding way, managed to foster both expectations of being liked, and expectations of success.

'When I went on to St Paul's, I found I had much better grounding than girls from other schools, many larger than Norland Place, but lesser in ideals. In the new jungle of St Paul's, I became very rebellious and aggressive. Eventually I was expelled.

'At Norland Place, there had been nothing to rebel against, nothing to fight about. It was a rule by love and trust and kindness, and it worked.'

When I won a scholarship to St Paul's Girls' School, the two head mistresses of Norland Place put their arms round me in their office, which was like a chintzy sitting room, and wept tears of joy. That was the sort of school it was, and I believe still is.

*

27

St Paul's was a different world, large and competitive and ruthlessly ambitious. Many people there would not have known a nanny if they saw one, unless she was their sister or aunt working for someone else.

The rough, bullying side of me, which had been gently kept down at Norland Place, came to the surface and enabled me to survive. Doady was thin and anaemic and still suffered dreadfully from a conscience, which might have been bearable if it had been about herself, but was usually fixated on the sins of others. She did not go about trying to convert people to virtue, but she suffered terribly on their behalf, while they went ahead and enjoyed their depravity. She had been safe in the tolerant, protective world of Norland Place, where you were allowed to be artistic, or slow or adenoidal, or brilliant, or idiosyncratic, or whatever you wanted to be. She had had her niche as a voluble and imaginative character with a passion for the truth.

She could not tolerate St Paul's, where nobody took any notice of her. So she thought, 'All right. I'll make them notice me. I'll be mad.' She went about being mad, and people used to come up to me and demand, 'I say, Dickens, is your sister ill, or what?' At one time, she put about the rumour that our mother was even madder than she was, chained to the wall of a padded cell.

I was still 'that clever little Monica'. They force fed me academically, and because I had to be the best, I ingested and digested it eagerly enough. As well as exams and the fiercely competitive sports, in which I also needed to excel, there was another major occupation for which I had not budgeted time: falling in love.

At this all-female school where the only man was Gustav Holst who taught music – how could he stand it? – with the great stress on achievement, and the pressures of a strict regime that made all of us very vulnerable to passion, I fell in love with Comfort Turner and Fiona Macleod and a big, thrilling girl whose name I can't remember.

One of the worthwhile lessons St Paul's taught me was how to get the most out of scaling the joys and plumbing the agonies of love. Later, when it was men causing the joys and agonies, many of the experiences – the eternal waiting for a glimpse of even the back of a head, the blackout of true vision of what the beloved is really like, the hope, the despair, the scheming for favours – were the same as those evoked by Comfort Turner, Fiona Macleod and Big Thriller.

Added to this already full life, I was also in love with horses. There were certain years during childhood and adolescence in which my whole week was geared towards Friday evenings, when we drove to Oxfordshire where the horses were. On Sundays when I left the reeking riding breeches to wait for me in the cottage bedroom and drove back in silence to London, I sat at the supper table, watering my soup with tears.

Again, even though I was a great girl of twelve or thirteen, Henry and Fanny did not say, 'Don't be an idiot.' They said, 'She's watering her soup with tears.'

3

All these events and circumstances, in fact the whole of my life until I went away to be a nurse at the start of the war, took place against the background of 52 Chepstow Villas, Bayswater, W.11.

It was a square double-fronted house, cleanly plastered all round except at the back, where it was surprisingly shabby, with dirty brown bricks, unpainted sills and naked water pipes.

In the paved front garden, plane trees and a few urban iris survived in gritty earth. A cutting from the American pillar rose at Chilworthy climbed languidly over the coal chute, and little saplings had rooted miraculously in tubs from seeds of fig and nespoli brought home from Italy. The wide steps, which the housemaid hearthstoned every day, were guarded by two granite Turkish cannon balls which Henry's brother Gerald had brought home from the Dardanelles in what we called the Great War until an even greater one arrived. The cannon balls were stolen in the nineteen sixties. I hope whoever took them dropped one on his foot.

The house was Victorian, solid but not grand, comfortable to live in, but inconvenient to run. Black dirt silted into the plaster mouldings round the high ceilings, which could only be reached with a ladder. The fogs of Kensington blurred the huge rattling windows. Every wall, even in the lavatories, was covered with framed enlargements of the photographs Henry took on the glass plates of his bulky old camera, which I lugged on my back, over the years, up and down Scottish hills and the lesser mountains of the Swiss Engadine. Henry's dressing room was miles away from the bathroom. Hot water had to be carried to him twice a day in a brass can with a lid. The basement kitchen was miles away from the dining room, with a nasty turn at the top of the stairs that was peril to a loaded tray.

Although it was not a mansion, but a fair-sized family house, it seemed to need a squad of maids to support life, as I remember it, at comfortable, unfashionable 52 Chepstow Villas.

At one time, when maids were getting hard to find for that inconvenient house of stairs and irregular plumbing, we had a manservant, who was part butler, part houseman. He was called Dowson. We never found out his first name. He made us all rather uncomfortable, but he poured wine with a napkin round the bottle, and knew about things like taking the butter off the table before he placed the port decanter at Henry's elbow.

The cut glass port decanter had a silver label which said that it was a prize from the North Kensington Lawn Tennis Club, where Henry, in yellowing white flannels and buckskin shoes, played mixed doubles while Fanny watched.

After her mid-forties, when I was about five, he would not play tennis nor dance with her, nor take her alone in a punt on the river at Sonning. She was expected to be, and was, friends with the younger women with whom he fox-trotted and punted and won port decanters. This sounds like philandering, but nobody saw it that way. They saw it as lovable old Hal, typically making his own laws. On the few occasions when I heard Fanny express resentment at their one-sidedness, she took it back quickly, conditioned, like all Dickens wives, to these tyrant-child sons of Marie Dickens, the salt of the earth. When I was sixteen, Fanny confided to me that it was a sad fact of life that a man was not interested 'that way' in his wife after she turned forty. She was thirty-nine when she had me. Whew! Just in time.

Henry's innocent carryings-on were part of the boyish mystique of his life, in which 'his' places, like the Tennis Club and the dance studios and the Golf Club and certain reaches of the Thames were sacred.

During the war, when the suave green courts were dug up for vegetables, the earthy bundles of carrots and celery that Henry flung down on the hall table for non-existent maids to clean, still had a whiff of sanctity, not only because he had grown them, but because they came from the hallowed earth of the North Kensington Lawn Tennis Club.

When I was a child, I thought the prize port decanter was a holy object, like the gold chalice in which the priest buried his nose on Sundays. The rituals of its clockwise movements in the dining room were as rigid as the Mass. There were other Henry rituals more esoteric, like the seven cut-throat razors marked for the days of the week, one Turkish cigarette in the lavatory after breakfast, and walking the length of the Underground platform at Notting Hill Gate to kick the end wall before the Inner Circle train came in. This was especially sanctified, since it took place on a Sunday en route to South Kensington and the Brompton Oratory.

On the way back, purified in your white socks and strap shoes, you were allowed to jump and screech and bellow at the echoes in the tunnel that led from Brompton Road to the station, going home to stump cricket with Henry's friends in the backyard of 52, followed by the ritual hot roast lunch that allowed the maids only half a day off on Sundays.

For our family of four, and five when my brother was at home, we had Miss Ellen Page, known as Mrs Page because she was the cook, Mary Lott, a large, good-humoured girl who was the house parlourmaid, Nanny Gathergood, Annie Bavin who came in to sew, and Roland Majer, an impeccable young man with clipped golden hair on the back of his neck, who chauffeured the Wolseley car.

Part of his job was to teach Henry and Fanny to drive. Fanny had her first lesson in the country, miles from anywhere. The only traffic was a herd of cows round a corner of the lane. She hit one cow in the head and another in the rear, and returned as a passenger, for ever. Henry got his driving licence – there were no tests in those days – and drove the car on Sundays.

Although there were already so many accidents in London that underground crossings were proposed – scorned in the Commons by an M.P. who said that people would not use them, since they associated subways with public lavatories – to the privileged car owners, driving was still a sport. Motorists bitterly resented the new traffic laws on the unspoken grounds that since driving was an upper class thing, safety could be left to manners, not rules. Henry and his friends called every garage man 'George', and said, 'Call me Sir' to policemen who stopped them for using the roads like a club. Majer, finishing his tea with Ellen and Mary Lott on a Monday morning, would sigh, 'Well, better go and polish out the scratches on the old bus.'

Most important of all at 52, in all the years it housed our family, was Minnie Maunder, beloved charwoman. Minnie had earlier lived with us as a cook, with her children and Daddy Maunder, a mysterious bed-ridden figure with a limp ginger moustache, in the basement front bedroom.

Min had left her Devon village with Daddy Maunder, a carpenter, when she was about fifteen. She had a round face, tiny squashed nose and eyes like kindly currants. Her hair was gathered up all round into a cushion on top of her head, with a button of bun skewered on top of that. She was Henry and Fanny's first maid when they married in 1904 after a long engagement. In those four years, they were not allowed to ride in a hansom cab together, and Henry refused to tell Fanny what Oscar Wilde had done until they left the church after their wedding. She asked him right away. Her parents, still wary of the struggling Catholic barrister, would not let her get married until they could afford two servants, and Minnie Maunder was one of those in the top flat in Moscow Road near the Greek Orthodox Church of Saint Sophia. Henry used to let down a basket on a string from the window, and the boy from the Moscow Arms put bottles of beer in it, to go with Minnie's sausage and mash.

Minnie could hardly read or write, but nobody could touch her roasts, her crisp and bursting sausages, her fried fish, her liver and bacon with the gravy like strong velvet. Her open-face sandwiches were a feature of the big New Year's Eve parties at 52. As broad as she was high in her best blacks and starched apron, she stood flushed behind the buffet, calling young cousins Lovey, and greeted by all the guests, in an age when most people noticed other people's servants – or even their own – no more than serving spoons.

After Daddy Maunder disappeared, seeming to melt away, rather than die, she moved out with her children and the collection of China from Belgium and France and Italy and anywhere the family had been on holiday. She came back comfortingly to live at 52 for a while during the war, and afterwards, until she was quite old, she still came to the house every day, toiling up Denbigh Road from the 15 bus on swollen legs, to dust what she could reach and polish silver at the kitchen table.

When she could no longer go out, she lived with her married daughter in a house off Harrow Road, where her territory was a fireside chair and a bed in a room she shared with her grandson and his bicycle. She died in a gloomy hospital where people went only to die, and there is left at the edge of her totally beautiful memory a feeling of having let her down.

Mary Lott was a child's delight, who would rather play games than work. She taught me whist and card tricks and some racy sayings like, 'What's the time? Half past kissing time, time to kiss again.'

Every year when Henry and Fanny went abroad, to 'the cure' for Henry's chronic rheumatism at Aix-les-Bains or Abano, to Lake Como where they had spent their honeymoon, or to Pontresina in the Swiss valley where they first met, Mary Lott and Minnie would shroud the furniture and their heads in cloths and go at the house like demons. It can't have been all that dirty, since they cleaned bits of it every day, but they had the chandelier down and in pieces, the rugs rolled, and all the books out of the shelves.

Henry used to say that Minnie put them back upside down on purpose. He would yell for her, 'Minnie, you wretched woman!' and, 'She's done it again!'

She did not mind. When I grew older and asked her, 'Why do you let him talk to you like that?' she said, 'He can't help it, poor darlin'.' To be a gentleman was to her as much a handicap as an advantage.

When he yelled at Mary Lott, 'What the devil have you done with my glasses?' Mary would yell back, 'I haven't touched the rotten things!'

'Nor you have.' He would find them in his pocket and smile.

'All right then.' Mary stood with her powerful arms akimbo, and nodded at him. 'Next time . . .'

Henry had three or four pairs of precarious rimless pince-nez for various purposes. When they were not lost, they fell off and smashed. I never went abroad with him without the crisis of his glasses fragmented in the Villa Carlotta or the steps of Santa Maria Degli Angeli, and cables sent to Callaghan's in Bond Street for emergency replacements. He never had enough pairs to allow for all the accidents. The cloud no bigger than a man's hand that hovered at the edge of all our holidays was the fear that he would break the last pair and we would all have to go home.

My brother's name was Gerald Henry Charles. Since everyone in the family had a nickname, he was known as Bunny.

Nine years older than me, he should have been a great influence on my childhood, but he was hardly ever there. When I was four, he was already a Naval cadet at Osborne in the Isle of Wight. He went from ship to ship, and all over the world. His leaves were much too short for him to be more than a visiting idol. Fifty-two revolved round him when he was at home, yawning on the dining room sofa with his ukelele, complaining that since it was too wet to play golf, there was no point in doing anything else.

He was easily frustrated. His expectations were high. His disappointments were profound. Henry and Fanny used to argue about whether they had spoiled him in the early days when he was their brilliant only child, bringing the house to its feet at six years old when he starred in Fanny's first production of *Rainbowland* and sang all his encores in different foreign accents.

But he was too lovable to be callel spoiled. Not selfish or demanding, but just expecting that things would go right for him, because he was charming and clever and funny, and people loved him.

He made me laugh, and I worked desperately to make him laugh. I could only perform antics and pull faces and parrot grown-up sayings to be precocious. He had a fund of up-to-date witty expressions like 'One rode a horse and the other rode a dendron,' and, 'Same to you with knobs on and brass fittings, in lacquer box, more highly coloured, five and six.' He counted, 'One, two, six', which seemed hilarious.

Summer holidays at the Hôtel de Bruges in Coq-sur-Mer were much more exciting when he was there, even only for a few days. I carried his golf clubs and ran after tennis balls for him, and went to the bar to fetch his big glass mug of beer. 'Un bock pour mon frère.'

For years, as well as going to Chilworthy, we went to the same hotel behind the low sand dunes of the Belgian coast, in a big noisy group of assorted family and friends and their children and nannies.

The Dickens family were great for clan holidays. There is a long narrative poem written by Fanny in 1906 about a mass sojourn in Paramé, paid for by Henry's father when Bunny was a baby.

> 'In Brittany, at Paramé
> The season was especially gay.
> And why? Because the great K.C.
> And all his lively familee
> Were basking 'neath the skies of France.
> It wasn't by the merest chance
> That they had all assembled there,
> The great K.C. had paid the fare.
> He had invited everyone,
> from Auntie, to the little Bun.'

'Auntie' was Georgina Hogarth, Charles Dickens's sister-in-law, who lived with him as his housekeeper after his separation from his wife.

The poem goes on to say that the waiters at Paramé were 'snuffy' until bribed, perhaps because the family were overwhelming. Henry's mother had once turned out the whole choir of a seaside church, so that her seven children could sing at Mass.

At Coq-sur-Mer, our family and friends took over the whole place. We thought it was delightful for the hotel to have us all there so jolly, but it must have been hell for the few other guests who managed to get rooms.

The Dickens party crowded the little tram cars that ran by the sandy golf course, and used their own children to caddy instead of the local boys. They dominated the annual tennis tournament, assuming that the Belgians were lucky to have their casual, haphazardly rigged tennis tournament taken over by the sporting and efficient British. Luckily the contest, now sportingly rigged in favour of the British, was usually won by the Belgians, although their choppy, cunning returns from halfway down the court were not comparable to the long sweeping baseline strokes that were de rigueur at the North Kensington Lawn Tennis Club.

On Saturday nights there was the Fête à Lanternes, in which the whole of Coq marched down to the beach behind the town band, carrying lighted Japanese lanterns. The parade, breezily restyled the Flambo Jambo, was also appropriated by the rowdy party from the Hôtel de Bruges, whose singing sometimes sounded to me like the men weaving up the Portobello Road from the Lord Nelson, when I was in the bunk under the window in Bunny's little front room, watching the plane tree leaves move across the street lamp.

When Bunny was at Coq, my days were a tussle to make him notice me. I forced myself to stay awake downstairs at night, but at nineteen or twenty, he was preoccupied with other people. Later, when I was in love with a pony, it mattered less. Nothing about Belgium mattered then anyway, because it was not Oxfordshire, where I wanted to be. I was dragged unwillingly across the Channel, with the merry travellers running a sweepstake on who would be sick first (odds-on favourite, Nanny Gathergood), and sulked in hollows of the dunes with my cousin Phoebe, who had not wanted to leave her guinea pig.

Years later on a holiday in Sweden, Bunny fell in love with my best friend Ann, who had come to spend the holiday with *me*. Only slightly older than me, she was much more mature.

Naively, I failed to understand that she had changed her ideas about who she was spending the holiday with. I was like the child in the song:

> 'There they are, the two of them on their own,
> In the parlour, alone, alone, alone.
> They've given me half a crown to run away and play.
> Eye-tee-iddle-tee, Eye-tee-iddle-tee ... Ay.'

But they gave me no half-crown, and at first they were too polite to tell me to run away and play. The moment when Ann was forced to round on me and tell me to stop tagging after them everywhere was one of those hurts which leave an indelible wound which you can uncover and morbidly inspect for years to come, like a badly healed surgical scar.

I was supposed to be happy when they got engaged, but I was murderous with jealousy. Of both of them. They were both mine. How dared they usurp each other?

Later, the engagement was broken, but so was my friendship with Ann.

One of the most meteoric and glamorous phases of Bunny was when he had one of the first small sports cars, an open M.G., with wire wheels that knocked off with a mallet, a strap round the bonnet, and a windscreen that opened flat in the rain, because there was no wiper. He let me drive it when he was at sea, and I was meteoric and glamorous, racing strangers through the revolutionary traffic lights on the new Great West Road.

When he wrote from China to tell me to deliver the car to a girl called Joy at Caversham, the old wound of his engagement to Ann stabbed and sickened me. But it was only because of the car, and jealousy was gone by the time of their marriage.

It lasted a little over a year, ending like a brief dream when Bunny was bitten by a malarial mosquito in the Canary Islands, and died on the cruiser H.M.S. *London*, and Joy came back to England to have their baby.

The most memorable thing about that grief is the way it

seemed to diminish everyone physically. Henry and Fanny immediately became much smaller, and Joy, staying at 52, crept inconspicuously about, although she was bigger with pregnancy, almost as if she did not exist.

4

After I was expelled from St Paul's School, I was sent to a finishing school in Paris, where we had to urinate out of the windows because they locked us in our rooms at night, and Madame tried to kill her daughter Yvonne with a kitchen knife, instead of teaching us to cook, which was what she was supposed to do.

I came back to be presented at Court, which was the thing that everybody did, to announce that you were Out. First you were a Flapper. Then you were Out. Then you had a few respectable romances with young men who owned their own suit of tails, and ended up at the altar of the Brompton Oratory, panic-stricken, but relieved at least of the greater panic of being on the shelf.

I don't believe Fanny wanted to go through the expensive charade any more than I did. Her younger sister Gerty had taken a house in Belgravia for Phoebe's Coming Out Season. Fanny was not envious or competitive, but she was suggestible. If vibrant, witty Gerty, who called Viscounts by their nicknames, pronounced that it was essential to my chances, then who were Fanny and I in Bayswater to say that it might not be?

Being presented meant wearing a pink satin gown with a swag of artificial roses over my overgrown bosom, and three feathers up the back of the head to please the Prince of Wales. With cheerful, boyish Majer at the wheel of Henry's blue Wolseley, we queued for hours on Constitution Hill among Rolls-Royces and Daimlers with hawk-nosed chauffeurs and coronets on the door. Fanny ate ham sandwiches from a brown paper bag. When we finally got into the Palace, she had to go to the ladies' room, which was chamber pots in curtained cubicles. The single minute we spent in the throne room, too scared to look at the bored Prince of Wales, deputizing for ailing George V, was not worth the price of curtseying lessons from Madam Vacani.

I was Out in the Season, which meant debutante balls and fork lunches and tea at the Ritz. I was invited here and there because I was on some second class list, but the deb dances were not much more thrilling than the Saturday night hops in the corrugated iron hall of the Oxfordshire village where we had our weekend cottage. In Britwell, the village girls sat on benches along one side of the hall and tried to look as though they were not waiting to be spoken for. At the Dorchester or the Hyde Park Hotel, the bright-lipped debutantes gossiped and giggled on gilt chairs and brocade sofas and tried to look as though they were not etc., etc.

Equal numbers of men were invited, but only the breath-smelling toe-steppers and poor relations came for the whole dance. The cream of youth came mostly for the suppers. They went from dance to dance, lapping up champagne and cramming lobster mousse and chaud-froid of chicken past those runaway chins which receded so decadently over their white ties.

After my season I drifted, achieving nothing, liking myself less than when I was a striving child. At twenty-one, I was an ageing and disgruntled ex-debutante. My girl friends were more attractive and sophisticated. And thinner. I weighed eleven stone and could not see my feet. My bosom ballooned in the hammocks that passed for bras in 1935. My thighs were like trees. We went to Quaglino's and the Savoy and the Berkeley and the Coconut Grove and a nightclub called Rector's. Since one had to be out every night of the week, any man who could afford it was acceptable, and I was too fat to be choosy. Only men who could not do better took me to Quag's and Rectum's and the new Ace of Spades on the Kingston by-pass.

When I had no one, I travelled secretly all over London to watch films in outlying cinemas. I saw all the Hollywood musicals, several times over, addictively. Dick Powell, Ruby Keeler, Eleanor Powell, Joan Blondell were my conspirators in obsession.

With a friend who lived in the Isle of Wight, I used to hang

41

around the Fleet at Portsmouth and Southsea, keeping out of the way of my brother if he was in port, and of my Uncle Gerald, who was captain of the battleship *Repulse*.

A painful memory is of us wearing boiler suits given to us by a stoker on a minesweeper and sailor's hats with 'H.M.S. *Dundalk*' on the ribbons. Ann was small and trim. I was – well, thank God there remains no photograph of me loaded into my boiler suit.

Another friend and I used to drive up to Oxford and Cambridge with a gramophone on the back seat of my Sunbeam SS, playing 'Jeepers Creepers' and 'You're an Old Smoothie'. Winding it while you drove was quite an art. We went to balls, and parties in people's rooms. We were very gay. It was at a Magdalen sherry party where I wore my blue ribbed jersey dress, that I overheard two fellows laughing at me from the other side of the room.

'Come up and see me some time,' they snickered, the slogan of Mae West. But it did not mean I was sexy. It meant that I was *fat*.

Like an alcoholic who is finally traumatized into the realization that something must be done, I asked Fanny for help.

'Just puppy fat,' people had been saying. 'She'll fine down.'

But Fanny saw that I was desperate. Glands were coming into style, and she took me to an endocrinologist, who said I was deficient in thyroid.

It was the miracle of my life. On a couple of thyroid pills a day, the bosom, the thighs, the thick rubbery waist began to melt away like Daddy Maunder. I weighed myself four times a day. Obsessed with getting thin, I ate less and less until I did not want food any more. Although my energy was fading along with the fat, I made myself walk all over London, in and out of shops, across the Park, along the Embankment. On days when I had only eaten a salad, I liked myself. On days when I had been seduced into eating a meal, I hated myself. Sometimes I would wake in the night so hungry that I would creep down to the kitchen past Ellen Page's snoring door, and gorge with fatty stuff, cakes, white bread, fried onions. Horrified, I would dose myself with castor oil to get rid of it. Finally, our family doctor discovered what was going on and threatened to put me in hospital and force feed me through the nose, like the Suffragettes.

The drama of it gratified my neurosis. Enough. I could stop short of nasal feeding. Cautiously, I began to eat. Energy returned, but I never got fat again.

My disposition improved. I no longer had to cross the street to avoid saying Hullo to someone. But fat or thin, I was still drifting. On Sundays when I had nothing to do, I walked in the Park with my big dog Ugly, whom I had rescued from a chain under a rainwater tank in a Cornish farmyard. Everybody else was with a boy friend, a husband, children. They passed without noticing me. Some day, I told myself, they'll know who I am. Why should they? The dream did not extend to ambition.

My sister had fallen in love in Farm Street Church and swiftly married a handsome vet who was the rage of Mayfair pet owners. My best friend had married a man she stole from me. My brother had married the girl he lent his M.G. to. Another friend got married. Cousins were getting engaged.

I would get a job. What as? I was trained for nothing. I had got myself expelled from St Paul's, not only because I was fed up with the uniform hat, a black felt bucket like a Mennonite preacher, but fed up with brainwork. I had won scholarships and got honours in exams. No one pushed me, and I cannot remember pushing myself, but at seventeen, I had had enough. I threw my gym tunic and the preacher's hat into the Thames off Hammersmith Bridge, and the High Mistress, inscrutable and stately Miss Strudwick, told Fanny that since I was not suited for University, I might try something civic, like a sanitary inspector.

What kind of job could I do? My brain had lain fallow since St Paul's. The only thing I had learned was a small amount of cooking. With some other fatuous debs, I had taken six lessons at the Petit Cordon Bleu school in Sloane Street, a fashionable thing to do, with no danger of being thought earnest.

There I had learned to poach eggs the French way, folding them into blobby packages in vinegared water, and to make a

43

tolerable *béarnaise* sauce. I can still do both. My *béarnaise* is much better since I discovered that you do not have to whip the butter cautiously into the eggs over a pan of hot water, or *bain marie*, as we said at the Cordon Bleu. You simply put the egg yolks and mustard and salt and pepper straight into a small pan over low direct heat, and whip in slowly very hot melted butter. If it curdles, you stir in an ice cube, and it comes out thick and creamy.

I thought I would be a cook. Apart from the Cordon Bleu, and a pedestrian place in Gloucester Road where I had learned to make rissoles, cooking looked like being the easiest thing to learn as one went along.

There was a domestic agency in Knightsbridge called Universal Aunts – now in Chelsea – which was famous for doing things that real aunts ought to be doing, like meeting small boys from India at the boat train and taking them across London to their train for school, with a stop for tea at Lyons or Gunters on the way. They also supplied servants. My mother had never got any there. She was in thrall to Mrs Lines in the Fulham Road, which was why I chose to go to Universal Aunts.

I took a 52 bus to Knightsbridge in a mackintosh and a round brown hat, as excited as if I were going for a tryst with a forbidden lover. I was going for a job. Nobody knew. No one had seen me go out except Minnie, on hands and knees like a Flemish mare, polishing the hall linoleum with Ronuk, and giving me the time-honoured Godspeed, 'Give him my love and tell him Yes' without even looking up.

Outside the Hyde Park Hotel, debutantes with big hats and hard orange mouths were going into a wedding. I had been one of them myself too many times, aimless, drifting, envious of the bride, even though the man she had got was not what I wanted. But I thought she had something that I wanted – a purpose, a status? I did not quite know what it was. Probably nor did she.

Universal Aunts was divided into sections for those who wanted a servant and those who wanted to be one. There were separate waiting rooms, in case people might get talking and strike up a deal and leave without paying the agency fee.

A kindly faced aunt faced me across a desk, a tea at Lyons aunt. I told her that I was a cook and was available to go out and cook people's dinners for them. Under her placid, accepting gaze, I felt I was a cook already.

'Dinner parties?'

'Yes.'

'Let's see ... a cook.' She looked through some papers. 'You are a good cook, are you?'

'I've had lessons at the Cordon Bleu.'

'That place in Sloane Street? I've been there for lunch. Their *rouget aubert* is delicious, and I always have the chocolate *mousse*.'

'Perhaps,' I dimpled, 'you've eaten something I cooked there.'

'Perhaps I have.' She looked up from the papers and smiled. She was being too kind to me. It was a bad sign. 'There's not much available, I'm afraid.'

The telephone rang. A duck quacked at the other end.

'Well, it's short notice. Thursday night? And the following week? Well ...' With the telephone to her ear, she puckered her brow at me, then took a breath of decision. 'As a matter of fact, I've got someone in the office who might be able to help out.' She put the receiver face down on the desk, which was easier to do when receivers were shaped like little trumpets. 'Would you be able to cook for a dinner party next Thursday?'

'How many people?'

'Twelve.'

'*Twelve?*' There are watershed moments in life, when you are either going to plunge on or drop back. 'I think so.'

The duck did not want to speak to me in the office. I was given a number to ring her. Sick with a mixture of dread and excitement, I went down the narrow stairs and crossed the road to the telephone box outside the post office.

'Mrs Carlson? I was at Universal Aunts. They said you needed a cook.'

'I've got a cook. But she's not very experienced. I want someone extra for the dinners.'

'Dinners?'

'For my brother. He's back from the East, and I want to make it special.'

'Special.'

'My table will only seat twelve, so I'm having two dinners. Are you sure you can manage that?' She sounded anxious, as well she might. 'We'll have the same menu.'

'What would that be, madam?' It was the first time I had said madam. It was like the first time those envied brides said Mrs in shops.

'We're going to have lobster cocktail, then soup, of course, then I thought some turbot, don't you know, with cheese sauce.'

'*Mornay.*' I grabbed my chance.

'That's right. And I have a brace of pheasant my cousin sent me from the north. They've been hanging. The fishmonger will dress them. Unless you'd like to?'

I let that go. 'And pudding, madam?'

'Oh, trifle. My brother always liked trifle.' Her voice smiled. *Sponge cake.* I saw Ellen Page at the kitchen table, tight-lipped, with her teeth in a vegetable dish on the dresser. *You put jam on it, then fruit and stuff, and make the custard. Ratafia biscuits . . .*

'We'll finish with a simple savoury.'

. . . almonds. Glacé cherries. How do you whip cream?

Mrs Carlson gave me the address in a north London suburb. 'I'll have everything bought. Cook will show you where things are.'

It would be better if she showed me how to cook.

'When will you be here? Come in good time.'

I had no idea what that would be. 'In good time.'

Mrs Carlson caught a whiff of my panic. 'Are you sure you can manage?'

I nodded, producing a wordless noise.

'I hope it will be all right.'

'So do I, madam.'

I left the telephone box and walked like a dreamer to the bus stop. Outside the Hyde Park Hotel, a few sated debutantes with top-hatted escorts were already straggling out, their orange and crimson lipstick slack with midday champagne. I felt light-years away from them. I had a job. I was a cook.

I rang the bell of the bus at the corner of Kensington Park Road and Chepstow Villas and ran the few yards to 52, and let myself in to that high familiar hall with the grandfather clock whose weights were pulled up by Henry every Sunday at exactly the same time. In the daytime, you were not aware of the clock's ticking. Coming home too late and jaded, trying to shut the heavy front door quietly, so that no one would wake and shout, 'Is that you, Monty?', the measured beat of the pendulum was like a clicking tongue and a wagging finger.

Sounds of lunch from behind the tall brown door of the dining room, and I heard the voices of two of my aunts, one Dickens, one Runge.

'She seems rather a common little person.' Sniff.

'Do you think so? I don't think so at *all*.'

Mary Lott came out with a tray laden with the mammoth tureens and dishes which she lugged up and down the kitchen stairs several times a day.

'Who else is there?' I jerked my head at the door, as she shut it with her heel.

Mary was not wearing the morning work dress, which she usually kept on for lunching aunts, but her white parlourmaid apron over her second-best blacks.

'Some old bag with a handle. Do you want lunch?'

'No thanks.' I was too excited to eat. I did not go into the dining room. I wanted to tell Fanny I was a cook, but not in front of the unknown bag with a handle, let alone the two aunts, who would relay it all round the family the next morning.

'Have you *heard* what that ridiculous Monica has done now?'

'Monty's a cook. My dear – *too* amusing.'

I had not minded my nickname in the days when my passion was to wear boy's shorts or riding breeches. Growing up, I began to hear it in the ears of other people, like suddenly seeing the ugliness of a familiar piece of furniture.

'Monty's a cook – too amusing.'

'But my dear, she can't cook.'

'I know. Isn't it priceless?'

'Well, no doubt Hal and Fanny are thankful she's finally doing *something* besides going about looking so common with all that stuff on her face.'

Being common was almost as big a crime in our family as being stupid.

At dinner, roast lamb, roast potatoes, boiled leeks, gravy, onion sauce and poor knights, Ellen Page's version of the German *arme Ritter* – rounds of fried bread with strawberry jam – I still did not tell Henry or Fanny. Not because they would ridicule or veto, but because the morning's excitement was beginning to metabolize into panic. *Arme Ritter?* I didn't even know how to fry bread.

After a night of waking in a sweat, trembling alternately from excitement and fear, I knew that I would not tell anyone yet. I would wait until it was over, and then astonish them with my tale of disaster or triumph.

The disaster began when I arrived at Mrs Carlson's much too late, because I had no idea how long anything took to prepare and cook, and ended at midnight when Mrs C. handed me three half-crowns and told me not to trouble to come back next week, since Cook had decided she could manage the dinner. After seeing me in action, she must have felt like Brillat-Savarin.

My turbot was coarse and dry and the sauce had separated. I had not known how to carve the pheasants. The trifle had been tasted and left on most of the plates. I had broken two glasses and a tureen lid and burned up a wooden spoon. But it didn't matter. *It didn't matter.* Although my ego was as crushed as the tip of the finger that had been eaten by the lobster tin, I knew now what I wanted to do, and where I wanted to be.

Mrs Carlson had hired a butler of a kind and two maids to serve my ill-starred meal. They were angry with me during dinner, because I did not have things ready, and the food looked as unpalatable as it was, and Mrs Carlson was making bulldog faces. But when it was over, we had been welded together in the common cause of us against them. The butler had kept back some wine, and I, green as I was, had known enough to reserve the best bits of pheasant. Ignoring the washing up, we had a charming little supper round the kitchen table, tearing apart the hostess and guests piece by piece, as I had torn those doomed pheasants with my hands when carving did not work.

At restaurants and dinner parties, I had always suspected that the waiters and the servants were having a better time than I was. It was true. I felt more at home in Mrs Carlson's kitchen than I ever had in any dining room upstairs, trying to make small talk from left to right, my legs twitching from boredom and one shoe mislaid under the table.

For twenty-one years I had lived above ground. Although Ellen Page and Minnie and Mary Lott and Majer were my friends, I had never really been more than a visitor below stairs. Now I belonged in that company.

Next morning, I put on the hat again, flagged down a 52 bus, and went back to Knightsbridge and the office of my universal aunt.

'What happened?' She had already been on the telephone with Mrs Carlson.

'Well – it was a mistake really, saying that I was a – a special sort of cook. I – well, you see. I thought I'd get more money.' Might as well come clean, even though I was lying. 'What I really am is just a cook. A cook-general, really.' I might be able to fool employers, but not other servants. Safer to be on my own.

'Bit young for a cook-general, aren't you?'

'My father's dead.' I made the right kind of face. 'I've always had to help.' I put my poor workworn hands under the desk, so she would not see how unused they were.

'What sort of jobs have you had?' An open question that deserved an open answer.

'I've had one or two places in the country.'

'References?'

'I can get them.' I had friends with good addresses on their parents' notepaper. They could write letters with invented names. By the time an employer got her request for a reference back: 'Not known at this address', I hoped to be so well established as a Treasure that it would not matter.

'Live in or out?' She opened a ledger.

'Oh.' I had not thought of living in. I was too comfortable at 52 Chepstow Villas. 'Out, I prefer.' I put on the face again. 'Since my mother's on her own . . .'

'Let's see.' She was leafing through the ledger. 'There is that job in South Kensington. No.' She looked up at me. 'I don't believe that would suit you.' She meant that I would not suit it, but was too auntly to say so. 'There are some others though. Cook-generals don't grow on trees these days. I'm sure we can find you something.'

5

The memory of the next two years is a bit confused between what actually happened and what I wrote about it later.

In those two years, I had about twenty jobs. They were easy to get in the late Thirties. Fewer people wanted to be servants, but until the war forced everyone to learn how to take care of themselves, just as many people still wanted them.

The family telephones did indeed report that it was too amusing, but after a while, it was not amusing any more. It was a fact of family life that Monty was eccentric again, and more or less lost to view.

The first risk the aunt took with me was an afternoon job on Campden Hill for a boring old couple of dried walnuts who never had any visitors, and only spoke about once an hour to each other, and almost never to me. All I had to do was get the tea, draw the curtains, wash the socks and underwear and prepare the dinner for the nutshell lady to cook. They mostly had shepherd's pie and diced carrots, so about the only things I learned there were that you can go on peeling an onion for ever, and that some people lead even more useless lives than I had. I did not think I would stay there very long.

The telephone rang in the hall at 52.

Dowson appeared sinisterly round the drawing room door, running his eye over the harmless company like a terrorist with a group of hostages.

'Telephone for Miss Monica,' he said, with the insulting inflection he always managed to give my name. God, I was afraid of that man.

When I came home late, and paused in the ticking hall to make sure everybody was asleep, I always felt that below me, in his rotten little bedroom beyond the scullery, Dowson knew exactly what time I came in and what I had been up to. When I lay awake under the window in what used to be the day nursery, I listened for slow footsteps, and watched for the embossed brass door handle to turn stealthily and admit Dowson in some nocturnal werewolf guise.

He intimidated everyone, I think. That was why he was not sacked sooner. Minnie had suspected him from the first, because he was willing to do housework. She said he was an escaped convict – 'Dowson is a convent' – and when he disappeared one day without a trace between lunch and teatime, she counted all the silver, and was disappointed to find it intact.

We had only one telephone, a large wooden affair on the wall under the coats.

'Are you still working for those people on Campden Hill?' It was my aunt from Universal.

'As a matter of fact . . .' I had not yet made up a good story to persuade her that I was not a dilettante. 'Actually, no.'

I thought she would chide me, but she said, 'Oh good. There's a job just turned up in West Kensington that I think might suit you.' She never said, 'that I think you could do', but that was what she meant.

'What is it?'

I could hear Dowson moving about by the butler's tray on a trestle outside the dining room. He liked to listen to telephone conversations.

'Cooking, serving, cleaning. General work. A small house off Warwick Crescent.'

'That sounds good. Yes . . . yes. I'll ring her up.'

'Don't you want to know what the wages are?' Aunt sounded a little amused.

'That's all right.' Dowson was coming towards me with a tray of glasses. 'I'll find out. I've got to go. Thanks very much.'

Dowson manoeuvred the tray deftly past me with a flick of

his sinewy hips, which was more suggestive than if he had brushed me.

When he had gone downstairs, I rang up Mrs – let's call her Cavendish. I can't remember the names of all my employers.

She was breathless with pleasure. 'You're free? Oh good.' The Campden Hill woman had never talked to me like that, even when she talked. Mrs Cavendish wanted me to go round right away.

'Yes, I'll come. Thank you very much.' As I added, 'Madam', I heard Dowson starting up the kitchen stairs, with his ears like jug handles.

'Where are you going?' Henry looked round from the cathedral-shaped wireless which he used to sit and watch, while it delivered concerts and the news. 'To a party?'

'In this coat? I'm going to see someone in the hospital.'

I still had not hold them about my new career. When I went to Campden Hill, they thought I was still going to the dressmaking class at the Polytechnic.

I took the 27 bus, which I had ridden each morning for years as a schoolgirl, getting off at Cadby Hall to hurtle through Brook Green and down the cloakroom steps of St Paul's with half a minute to spare. Today I got off at the corner of Warwick Gardens, walked in mounting apprehension along a comfortable curve of family houses, and poked about in the backwaters of Edwardes Square and Pembroke Gardens, until I found Pembroke Studios.

Having no maid, Mrs Cavendish opened the door. She was in her thirties, effectively dressed and made up, and with a touch of that heady stuff which came east from Hollywood and we called it glamour.

She was surprised to see me, fair, tall and somewhat naive in a grey flannel suit, one of a pair my Isle of Wight friend and I had made at the Polytechnic in our misguided desire to dress our totally different shapes and personalities alike.

'Miss – er?'

'Dixon.' My subtle incognito. It had a voice to go with it.

'I'm glad you've come.'

Mrs Cavendish hired me on the spot, or as soon as she had taken me down the narrow hall into the kitchen, to run my professional eye over the stove and the matched storage jars and yellow gingham curtains.

People were so desperate to get help from the dwindling servant ranks that I never went after a job I did not get, often because I was the only applicant.

Because she lived in a studio and was glamorous, I thought that Mrs Cavendish might be a painter. But she did not seem to be anything. Her day started with breakfast in bed with the papers and her letters. She got up slow and easy, with reading in the bath mid clouds of talcum powder which I had to remove from horizontal surfaces later with a damp sponge. Once dressed, she was either out seeing people or at home with people coming to her.

I liked it better when she was out in the morning, so that I could somehow invent my way through the housework unobserved. A vivid Cavendish memory: I put polish on the hall floor without rubbing it in, carried up the coal bucket, slipped on the polish, put out a hand to save myself, scrubbed at wall to remove hand smudge, found out that wallpaper is not washable, moved grandfather clock two feet to hide disaster, found wallpaper a different colour behind clock, moved high-backed chair from drawing room to hide different colour wallpaper. 'Why have you moved that chair, Monica?' 'We must have somewhere to lay coats. The stand is broken.' Broke two pegs off the coat-stand to prove it.

One thing I learned from Mrs Cavendish, apart from how to put on make up, which I watched her doing while I was making the bed and dusting her knicks and knacks, was how to make a soufflé. My strength was good plain cooking, I had told her, after I discovered that she would not often ask me for good plain cooking. She was willing to add to my repertoire of fantasy feasts – 'Ah, the roasts we used to have at Her Ladyship's, my Yorkshire you wouldn't believe' – with things like omelettes and quiches and soufflés, that I might have learned at the Cordon Bleu if I had not got stuck with chocolate mousse and bearnaise sauce.

At Mrs Cavendish's, I was finding that with cooking, as with so many other things in life, you can bluff your way through either with unprovable excuses – 'That was the way they liked their haddock at the Hall' – or by answering 'I think so' to, 'Do you know how to . . .' and then going off to find out.

'You never made a soufflé at Her Ladyship's?' Mrs Cavendish's pencil-plucked eyebrows rose. 'What kind of woman was she?'

'She was a very nice lady. Still is, for all I know.'

'I should have thought that when the Finch-Pargeters came to dinner in the Rolls, or it was the Bishop's birthday . . .' She enjoyed the mythology of my former employers. They were more real to her than they were to me.

'They were mad for the plain things. As I've told you, madam, it was roasts, roasts, roasts. And in that kitchen, you wouldn't risk a soufflé, not with that old oven, you wouldn't.'

'But didn't they have quenelles in Mayfair?'

One of my memories was, 'When I worked in Mayfair', names unspecified, with a suggestion that they might be recognized.

'In Mayfair, I was the nursery cook, you see. We had our own little kitchen. In Monsieur Alix's kitchen, it would have been my life if I'd so much as picked up one of his whisks.'

It was fun, for both of us. If Mrs Cavendish knew that it was fairy tales, she never said so. She enjoyed teaching me – she was actually better than I was, but I was paid to be the cook – and my famous cheese soufflé became the sign of grace to be bestowed on Mr Freddie, or the Major, or Mr P. V. Rogers, when they were in favour.

Mr Freddie had rather an up and down time of it. He was in the wane of his cycle, and due to get his walking papers pretty soon, you could see that, but not until Mrs Cavendish was sure of the elusive Major, of the nifty pointed jodhpur boot and the last-minute cancellation.

The other thing I learned from the job with Mrs Cavendish

was that assaulting maids behind the scenes did not cease with the Victorians. When my employer happened on a little wrestling match in the pantry where Mr Freddie had come to get glasses, I got my walking papers before he did.

Working my way by slow degrees towards Mayfair, my next job was in Ovington Street, behind the Harrods garage where cars and chauffeurs waited until the commissionaire summoned them on the intercom.

My employer was Derek Patmore, a willowy young man who was an interior decorator and lived with his mother. It was his property, I think, but it was she who ran the small, tall terrace house, which was being done over and interiorly decorated at the time I was hired.

At Mrs Cavendish's, I had had it pretty snug. True, she was demanding about her soufflés and her furniture polish and the way I ironed her camiknickers, but I was often upstairs with her, and she talked to me. I was not a total troglodyte.

Derek was vaguely pleasant, and his mother might have been all right if she had ever been a servant and known what you can expect. It was here in Ovington Street that I found out why people were not able to get servants any more.

A typical day at the Patmores:

Dowson was supposed to bring up my breakfast, but I was up and away too early for him. I ran down the Portobello Road to the garage where we kept our cars, manoeuvred Henry's grey box on wheels so I could get my little car out, backed grey box in again, drove my Sunbeam across the Park and left it round the corner from Ovington Street, where the Patmores could not see that their cook-general had a car. It would have been simpler to take a bus, but I often left work so late that I needed the car to get home.

Down the area steps, stumbling under and over the workmen's planks and piles of rubble and paint tins. I picked up the milk and let myself in to the mess of the kitchen I had left last night, riddled me boiler, poured in coke with a roar that woke Mrs Patmore, put on the kettle and had her tea and hot lemon juice upstairs by seven-thirty. She had a nasty little dog with teeth like a rat which slept in her bed. The only good thing about it sleeping under the covers was that it took it too long to struggle out and attack me before I had drawn the curtains and left the room.

Derek's tea and Hovis did not go up until eight-fifteen, after the papers and the post had come. With the window closed and one bar of the electric fire stewing the vapours of sleep and men's shoes, I stayed no longer with him than with Mrs P. and her bandicoot.

Back down to clean up kitchen, dust dining room, lay breakfast, cook breakfast, serve breakfast, make tea for workmen, clear breakfast, wash up breakfast, receive Mrs P. in kitchen for day's meal orders, do one bedroom, make tea for workmen's elevenses, receive baker at back door, do other bedroom, answer back door bell to butcher, dust and hoover drawing room, back downstairs for grocer (my favourite), make tea and sandwiches for workmen's lunch, start upstairs lunch, serve first course, change back into cooking apron to fry *arme Ritter*, equally popular on this side of the Park, clear and wash up lunch, eat anything that was left, quick doze with feet on table, shocked awake by Mrs Patmore's bell.

'I have some guests coming to tea, so we'll need scones, and perhaps you could manage a cake.'

'It's a bit late for a cake, madam. The gas pressure is low.'

'Well then, you could run to the pastry shop in Walton Street and get something nice. Take little Frisky with you.'

I was supposed to have free time in the afternoons. But you did not say, 'I'm off duty, madam', and refuse to put your shoes back on. If people came to tea, or you had a long dinner to prepare, free afternoons were a fiction merely.

I hauled Frisky off to Walton Street, making cats' cradles of the lead and my legs as she crossed from smell to smell, then came home and made scone dough, left some of it on the door handle when the florist arrived, served the tea in my brown afternoon dress and muslin apron, put on my cooking wrap-around, trussed the chicken, peeled potatoes, strung the beans, said Goodbye to workmen, said No to workmen, answered upstairs bell to draw curtains and make up fire, back down to cooking, into black dress and frilled apron, stuck pins into cap just in time to answer bell to first dinner guest.

If you are the parlourmaid as well as the cook, it's all go. You cannot go upstairs in your cooking apron, and you cannot cook in your parlourmaid apron, and every time you start a delicate operation like hollandaise, the bell goes off like a cerebral accident above your right ear and you have to go upstairs. I wish I had known then about the ice cube technique. Not that we had much ice in my early days at the Patmores'. I had never seen a refrigerator before. Fifty-two had not got around to the new miracle, and nor had Mrs Cavendish. I treated the Patmores' little fridge like an extra cupboard, and used to leave the door open to save trouble, until the knowledgeable grocer explained to me why everything inside was melting.

I enjoyed dinner parties, but after I had cooked, served, and cleared the dinner, picked dishes and plates off the kitchen floor where I had dumped them between courses, and done all I could stand of the washing up, it was often after eleven before I hung up the stained overall, put on the old mac and climbed the area steps with the empty milk bottles, pretending I did not hear the drawing room bell asking me to make a pot of tea.

I had half a day off on Thursdays and Sundays, cut into by delaying lunch demands. Raw and clumsy as I was, the world's spiller and smasher, I think I gave fairly good measure for twenty-five shillings a week.

One compensation for the drudgery of the Patmores was the company of the workmen, comedians all. When I broke a dish or set the oven cloth on fire or let the potatoes boil over and fill the basement with unlit gas, the cry would go up, 'She's at it again!'

I was a sort of fool or mascot to them. 'There she goes,' they would say, as I fell off the stepladder or burned the toast. 'Marvellous, innit?' They created elaborate jokes for each other and me: a kipper tied to the exhaust of Paddy's motorbike, which cooked as he went home, a crossing of wires in the switch box so that all the bells in the house rang at once, a fish's eye looking at me from a slab of margarine.

The other pleasure was the social life of the back door. Mrs P. did trot out to the Kensington shops once in a while, or finnick round the grocery department at Harrods, making the courtly assistant bring items one by one for her inspection, as if they were jewels. But most of the food was ordered by telephone and delivered.

My friend the grocer came twice a day, first for orders with his pad and sucked pencil, and back in time for elevenses with the goods in the basket of his bicycle. He was very kind to me. He rumbled me on the very first day, when I did not know what shortening meant.

'Where's Alice then?'

'I don't know.' The only evidence of a former maid was a two inch black crust on the bottom of the oven.

'Ah, I didn't think she'd last much longer. Where did they find you then?'

I did not have to give him the widowed mother tale, nor Her Ladyship at the Hall. I gave him the truth, and he took me in hand and taught me many things about survival downstairs, including where Mrs P. had hidden the cooking sherry.

She only got it out when I was to make trifle or Newburg sauce. That sherry became the most watered bottle you could ever see, except for the medicinal brandy on Queen Mary ward at the hospital where I nursed during the war.

One or two of my friends had found out where I was, and took to dropping down to my kitchen when the coast was clear. Although I was exhausted, they persuaded me to go out again to parties and night clubs on my free evenings. Drooping over the mirrored dance floor of the Gargoyle Club, dozing at a dark corner table at the Coconut Grove . . . but you never went home until three or four, even if you were not having any fun. It was deathly to get up two hours later and face the boiler and the debris of the Patmores' cold supper, abandoned in the dining room, as if they had no legs to carry it down to the kitchen.

I was running out of steam. It was time to make a change. I

told Mrs Patmore that the job was too much for one person, and she retaliated by telling me that it depended who that one person was. We had not had open war before, but now, with me kneeling in the drawing room grate, holding up last Sunday's paper to try to make the fire draw, we began to get ancient petty grievances off our chests.

That time the gravy was all fat . . . I can't stand the bells . . . You're very slow . . . not enough time off . . . who broke that Meissen vase . . . It's bells, bells, bells . . .

Poor Derek drifted innocently in just as we were giving each other two weeks' notice. He tried to pour oil, but having glimpsed the idea that I need not be the Patmores' cook-general for ever, I could not wait for freedom.

The next afternoon when they were out, I left everything tidy, with a nice stew maturing in the oven, and a poem under the flour shaker with the wages Mrs P. had given me yesterday, before we started war.

6

I did not go back to Universal Aunts, because I had heard Mrs Patmore on the telephone about me. I did some temporary jobs for another agency – extra cook, cocktail and banquet waitress, daily woman, whatever I could get that did not tie me down. I wanted to catch my breath before I became someone's Treasure again. Once or twice at cocktail parties, I saw someone I knew and had to hide behind a palm, or keep my head down as I cruised the crowd with my tray of sidecars and white ladies. No one recognized me. If you are dressed in a frilled white apron with a starched cap worn either like a halo or a visor, according to what your hair is doing that day, people don't look at you as anyone they might possibly know.

Two more of my friends got married. My sister had a baby. I needed a niche. An aunt on the shelf, I went back to my Universal one.

'Where have you been?' she asked. 'Have you been working?'

'Not exactly.' As difficult to tell your agency you have been unfaithful as to admit to dabbling with a second therapist. 'My sister had a baby. I've been helping her to take care of it. Him.'

'Is that finished?'

I nodded.

'Good,' she said tartly, as if she disapproved of doing domestic work for nothing. 'I've got something for you. I gave it to someone else, but it doesn't seem to be working out.' That was usually a warning. 'The lady is an actress.'

An actress. I saw myself at the stage door, arriving with costumes and greasepaint. In no time at all, I would be her beloved dresser.

The lady was a well-known actress, whom I shall call Elektra.

I had seen her in a couple of plays, strong, gifted, beautiful, far out of reach. To call on her socially would have been unthinkable. To go with my Dixon hat and voice, applying for the job, that was different.

When you go after a job as cook-general, you may be invited to sit in a chair, and even have a cup of tea, if it happens to be there. If you get the job, you never sit down with your employer again. Summoned, you stand for orders, dressings down, or praise.

'Dinner was excellent last night.'

'Thank you, madam.' Alert. Hands behind back.

'People particularly liked the duck sauce. Mrs Quimby wants your recipe.'

'I'm afraid it's a secret.' I have no idea why it came out so well.

'The plates could have been warmer though.'

'Yes, madam.'

'And what happened to the savoury?'

'I don't know, madam.' Arms folded in front, weight on heels, stomach stuck out.

'Yes, well. I've got three people for lunch. I thought we might have veal cutlets. What are you doing at the moment?'

'Turning out the spare room.' My head's not tied up in a scarf for nothing.

'I'm frantically busy, so if you could just pop round the corner and get eight nice small cutlets and some of these dear little frills that go on the ends, you always make them so pretty.'

You don't woo me that way, madam.

'And that spinach soufflé you do so well. If you've got time.'

'I'll try, madam.' One hand propping up front of apron, the other out for balance on an occasional table. 'No harm done.' Putting back the fallen ornament, turned round so she can't see the chip.

Elektra sat me down in an armchair in her flat in Westbourne Terrace and gave me coffee. As I came into the room, something had scuttled out at the other end. It was like just glimpsing a mouse as you open a cereal cupboard.

We liked each other. Elektra made me laugh, and I thought that as long as I could make her laugh, that deep, huskily amused chuckle, I might get by.

It was good to be back in routine again, with the same place to go when you got up in the morning. Although I had rebelled in the end, one of the things I had liked about school was knowing where you were going every morning, and what you would wear. There is a secure, comforting rhythm to that, which is how they keep people in the Services.

Being a cook-general for Elektra was somewhat the same as for Mrs Cavendish and the Patmores, but more companionable. With the kitchen on the same level, I was not so isolated. The work was cleaning and cooking and serving and washing up and laundry. I was never asked to take her make up to the stage door, and understudy at the last minute for the maid who opens the play by drawing the curtains and letting in artificial daylight. The nearest I got to the theatre was seeing her in the romantic flounced nightdress she had worn in her last play when I took in her breakfast tray.

The first day I was there, I discovered who the mouse was. As I was washing up last night's dinner, a little old lady in a hair net and kimono came round the edge of the door, hanging on to it as if she were walking round the edge of a swimming pool.

'Can I help you?'

She jumped. 'Are you the new – er –'

'Shall I get you some breakfast?'

'Oh no, don't bother. Don't ever bother about me. I'll just get myself a cup of tea.'

She fiddled around, filling the kettle with enough cold water for an army, pottering about, laying herself a little tray, burning the toast, dropping the butter knife. 'No, I'll do it. There, I'll just dip it in your washing-up water. I don't want to give any trouble. I can manage for myself.'

It was Elektra's mother, back from the Orient a widow, and living with her for a while.

Her daughter was not domineering with her, but the mother

behaved as if she were. When friends dropped in, she would get up with a little cry and shut herself away like Mrs Rochester at Thornfield, and have to be called out of her room so she would not feel excluded.

'I'm not dressed, dear.'

'Well, come as you are.'

She would be so long dressing and wondering if she looked all right that the friends would be gone, or just going, and have to sit down all over again so as not to be rude.

At meals, if I went to her first with the entrée dish, she would whisper, 'Serve the guests first', or, 'Serve my daughter first.'

When she had finished disturbing my technique and embarrassing the guests, and was about to make a timid attack on her cooling food, someone would raise a point, and Elektra would send me off for a volume of Shakespeare or Sheridan, and everybody would have to stop eating while she stood up and declaimed. She declaimed powerfully and well, but I had brought in the potato soufflé and it was collapsing on the sideboard.

A famous, stuffily respectable writer was a frequent guest, more often for dinner than for lunch. Sometimes for breakfast too. I would whistle and bang up the outside staircase – maids did not use the lift – and let myself into the kitchen door to find a note on the tea trolley: '2 for breakfast'. Behind the door that led into the hall, the writer's grubby raincoat hung like a shed skin.

On cold mornings, I had to light a fire in my employer's bedroom before she would sit up and have breakfast. I was kneeling in the grate, sweeping up ashes and Balkan Sobranie butts, when the mound of Elektra heaved over in the bed. I looked round to see her great tragic eyes staring between the wild hair and the sheet.

'Monica,' she intoned in her deepest bass. 'I'm going to have to let that gentleman go.'

'Oh yes, madam?' Not my place to show surprise. 'Why is that?'

'He's a prig in bed.'

I liked being with Elektra, but any job got boring when the novelty wore off. After a few months, I was ready to move on. We had had a few rows, when she was stormy and I was sulky, and the final break took place in the kitchen, with words and wooden spoons flying, and the mouse looking round the door to say, 'The bathwater's cold, but don't anyone bother about me.'

Years later, I saw Elektra in a restaurant. I smiled. She stared for a moment, then smiled back politely but blankly. After a while, she came over and said, 'It's driving me insane. I know you quite well from somewhere, but I can't remember where.'

'In your kitchen,' I said. 'You sacked me.'

She broke into a shout of laughter that made people look up from their osso bucco and fake canelloni. 'I didn't sack you. You walked out.'

We could not remember what had actually happened, except that it had probably been a good idea.

I went to a family for a while, where there were children. I learned to make chicken rissoles and blancmange like white eyeballs, and the children learned to play whist and vingt-et-un round my kitchen table, as I had learned in the kitchen of 52. I went to boring people and entertaining people, to people who ate too much – disgusting, and too little – why am I breaking my heart over a hot stove?

In the two years I was a cook-general, I had about twenty jobs. You can stand anything as long as you know it's not for ever, and some of the places I worked in were pretty hard to stand. Servants may have been a dying race, but I had employers who behaved as if they had a multitude of starving serfs to draw from.

I had given up talking about my work at home. No one would listen any more. When I complained, they said, 'Why don't you give it up?' But I couldn't. I went on being a cook-general. It was all I knew.

I did not stay anywhere very long. When I got fed up, I would ring up my compassionate aunt and say, 'I can't stand these people any longer. What else have you got?'

She had couples and singles and old fussy people and country houses where you could shell peas on the doorstep, and London houses where you could count fifty steps from kitchen to nursery. And then I was back in the land of my novitiate with a job near Warwick Gardens. On my way to the interview, I passed the back of Pembroke Studios, and the gate that led into Mrs Cavendish's slot of back garden. The kitchen back door opened, and the head of a mop came out and agitated wildly in the bright morning, sending dust and flicks of paper and mop string spinning against the sun. The woman attached to the mop was large and slovenly, slopping out above and below apron strings, a hank of grey hair in her eye. I bet Mrs Cavendish never had any trouble with her being pinched in the pantry.

I climbed the front steps of a small square house, freshly plastered and painted, with blue window boxes planted by a florist. The only time you use the front door is for your interview, or when you are hearthstoning the steps.

Mrs Fisher was a bride. She was one of those debs I had envied at Mayfair weddings, except that she was married in the country, walking on her father's arm from the Manor to the little church, with respectful villagers mowing and mopping as she went by.

'Isn't she lovely?' they sighed, as well they might. She was a beautiful girl, with a fresh, credulous face within a daffodil bell of hair. Her husband Mervyn had soft black hair and anxious wrinkles. He had just started to work in one of those socially acceptable banks that have a family name, but he had stayed at home for the interview because Marion was nervous.

She was nervous of me before she even saw me. The mere idea of my being her cook had set her fair skin flushing and blushing and her pony club hands folding and unfolding in the lap of her soft wool skirt. After their honeymoon, they had stayed with friends until their new house was ready. She had never employed anyone before. She told me this with her first breath. One down to her if we had been playing the usual game of mistress and maid. Although we were the same age, I felt like a kindly veteran.

'My mother wanted to come down from Warwickshire and help with the interview.' She screwed up her pink mouth a little, and her husband, who was standing behind her like a Victorian portrait, tightened his hand on her shoulder.

'I'm sure that's not necessary.' I smiled in my kindly way. 'I'm sure you and I can come to a good understanding.' I had already decided I was going to work here.

Marion did not ask me any of the right questions, so I gave her the answers anyway, to pass on to her mother. Which she did as soon as I left. As I passed the front window, I saw her already lifting the receiver excitedly.

I went home and got my overall, my parlourmaid uniform, my afternoon dress with the café-au-lait set of apron, cuffs and cap, and my dear old shoes, and came back to cook dinner for them that evening.

I remember it as if it was yesterday. I stopped at the butcher's on the way and bought some gizzards and wings and made a lovely chicken broth for them. I floated some bread on the top to soak up the fat and then ate the bread. Oh, blessed thyroid extract which made such things allowable. They had a nice bit of fish, which she had been all the way to Harrods to buy – she never shopped anywhere but Harrods or Fortnums, with an occasional side trip to Barkers for mundane things like salt and brussels sprouts – tinned new potatoes and petits pois. When I opened her cupboards and saw what kind of stores she had, I wished I had asked for a higher wage.

For afters they had – what else? – *arme Ritter*, my best poor knights, light and crisp to convince them that they had found their domestic treasure, who would be baking bread before they knew what was happening, and twenty mothers from Warwickshire could not have found better.

Mum came down, of course, within three days, to view this jewel. She was nicer than I expected, small and downy-skinned. Not bossy. Her daughter would be just like her in thirty years' time. She brought us vegetables from her kitchen garden, and I made a salad for their lunch with the remains of last night's chicken. Afterwards the mother did interview me a bit when

Marion was out of the room, asking me where I had worked, and so on. She then confided to me that her daughter was pregnant, which I knew, and charged me with the safe keeping of mother and child.

I took care of Marion and her baby and Mervyn and his lost socks and shirt buttons and fancy for crumpets and dripping at teatime. I enjoyed the intimate little dinners I staged in the miniature dining room the architect had concocted downstairs out of what had been the servants' sitting room. We had some elegant dinner parties too, with Marion's fresh-faced chums and their smooth pink husbands or boy friends, with perhaps an uncle or older family friend as a benevolent makeweight, to compliment Mervyn on his small cellar which was in my broom cupboard under the stairs. Uncle never knew that it was I who opened the claret and let it breathe over the potato steam, and I who showed Mervyn how to pour with that little wine steward's twist taught me by the grocer at the Patmores who used to be with the P & O.

As time went on, I began to be treated, as they say, like one of the family. People spoke to me as I was handing round dishes, and made little safe jokes.

'Aha, we're honoured tonight. Monica's Yorkshire pudding.'

'It's sensational. Ours always *collapses*. Utterly. How do you get it so light?'

'I blow into it, Lady Sheila.' I was allowed to joke back.

As I handed round the bronxes before dinner: 'This is Monica.' Marion drinking orangeade. 'We couldn't live without her.'

'Ooh, aren't you lucky? I can never get anybody who stays.'

'Well,' says the kindly old retainer, 'of course a lady like Mrs Fisher would never have any difficulty getting anybody to stay'.

'Oh shut up, Monica.' The breathless boarding school gabble. 'She hates us really. How is dinner? Is it going to be a success?'

Sometimes it was a failure. Two years had not made me fool proof. If it was a failure, they opened a terrine of foie gras and had boiled eggs and champagne.

The only fly in that jar of cold cream which was the household of Mervyn and Marion Fisher was my enemy that stood in the south-west corner of the kitchen. I had had some practice with the boilers that sulked in the kitchens of the Thirties, but when this one put its mind to it, neither methylated spirits, lighter fuel, nor even once a desperate slug of gin would get it going.

Every night I would bank the bloody thing up with a nice hodful of coke. Every morning the bloody thing had gone out and Mervyn could not have his bath. The word bloody is literal. When you had your hand inside, erecting a Boy Scout structure of paper and wood and choice bits of coal, the damper had a nasty way of falling down on your knuckles. The cast iron of that boiler was stained with my life's fluids.

Life went on unremarkably. I settled into a rut. There was nothing to complain about, and I had no energy to change jobs anyway. Getting up early to struggle with the boiler, and often getting home late after dinner parties, I was too exhausted to do much more than sleep on my half days and Sundays off. My friends no longer thought it fun to visit me in the kitchen. No one invited me to the theatre, because I always fell asleep before the first interval. At home, I was tired and bad-tempered, almost back to my pre-thyroid days.

I might have remained downstairs for ever. I was too apathetic to look much farther ahead than when the sweep was expected, and whether to have the silverside on Thursdays, or keep it for Saturday lunch.

And yet something was stirring besides my wooden gravy spoon. Since its over-exposure at St Paul's, my brain had gone to ground. But now the hibernating monster was twitching in its sleep. It may have been the long-term effect of the thyroid. It may have been that a late-maturing person was finally, at twenty-three, almost grown up. One day, with the same sense of discovery with which I had thought, 'I'll have a job', I thought, 'I'll use my brain.'

Nowadays, everybody who can't write writes a self-help book.

In those days, they all wrote cook books. That was what I would do, out of my vast knowledge accumulated through experiments, disasters, second degree burns and wastage of food in other people's kitchens. How could I make it different from the books of all those other women who had been doing the same thing since Charles Dickens's wife Catherine Hogarth wrote *What Shall We Have For Dinner?*

Ever since I could remember, Fanny had been writing poetry. She and I could write a cook book in verse and make enough to buy ourselves a little gas water heater for the coffin-shaped bath at 52, where the boiler, though easier to light than the Fishers', yielded nothing over a hundred and twenty degrees.

Nothing remains of her contribution. Of the entries I sketched out on my day off, I remember:

> 'Here's a thing you'll not forget.
> Never beat an omel*ette*.
>
> Cook sausage slowly, keep it moving,
> Thus the flavour much improving.
>
> If the grains of rice could talk,
> They'd clamour, "Stir us with a fork." '

It was probably just as well that I wrote *One Pair of Hands* instead.

It was the Firemen's Ball at the Paddington Baths, with boards laid over the Mixed Swimming bath. A friend who lived near the baths invited me to a dinner party before the ball, where we would do the Paul Jones and the Palais Glide – too democratic.

I did not want to go. I had nothing to wear. I was too tired, and it was not my night off anyway. When I heard that one of the guests was a young man from a publishing firm, I changed my night off. Marion did not mind. She was working on a cook book entry on bread and milk:

> 'It's clear that you must
> Leave on the crust.'

She wanted to see it in print.

Recent memory replays like a film. For instance, if I think of our Christmas party last year, I see movement and colour and hair as people mill about, hands raised in greeting, a head thrown back in laughter. There are babies and doting women on the kitchen floor, bent backs converging on the bread and cheese like grackles at the bird feeder, the swirl of a skirt as the piano starts and someone dances, the young girls of my family moving through the crowd with their bright beautiful faces among the middle-aged. Far off memory comes more in stills than moving pictures. Of a whole chunk of your life, you may be left with a few stock shots, motion arrested, to capture the essence of a span of time.

That whole evening of the Firemen's Ball is nailed in my mind's gallery in two images. In one, I sit next to the man from the publisher's at dinner and tell him I am writing a cook book in verse, and he changes the subject quickly. In the other, we sit on a lumpy settee behind a tiled swimming bath pillar and he asks, looking at my hands, 'What do you do?'

I told him. He listened. Years later his wife, who was then his fiancée, told me that she had gone home alone in a pique.

Charles Pick, who is still my publisher at William Heinemann, was then a young London salesman for Michael Joseph. He already showed the infectious Svengali enthusiasm to which many writers beside me owe the fact that they have had the courage to go on writing.

'I want you to come and talk to M.J.,' he said.

'About the cook book?'

'No, no, no.' The impatient sideways gesture of the hand with which he shoos off idiotic suggestions, or people introducing red herrings. 'About all this. You ought to write a book about what you've been doing.'

I felt vague, but on my next free afternoon I went to Bloomsbury Street, though scarcely knowing what for.

Michael Joseph was more specific. 'If you'll write a book about being a cook-general, we'll publish it.'

He gave me a contract before I had written a word. I thought that was what happened to all new authors. Someone begged you to write, and you wrote.

'Suppose I can't write?'

Michael, who seemed like a father figure to me, although he was not yet forty, gave me the most persuasive smile from his repertoire of charmers and said, 'Well then, you just tell us the story, my dear, and we'll write it.'

If that was how it was going to be . . . On the wall of his office was a filmy, dreaming picture of the young Daphne du Maurier, who had just written *Rebecca*: 'To Michael, with love.'

'I'll do it myself.'

Giving my notice to Marion was difficult. She was about six months gone, and a bit weepy. I cannot remember the reasons I gave. I probably told her what had already been on my mind, that I could not stay when the monthly nurse came to the house, and reorganized what was now my citadel.

She wept. Her mother came down from Warwickshire to give me a straight talk. Mervyn gave me the doggy look he wore for pattering down the back stairs in his dressing gown to ask when the bathwater would be hot. All I could do, with the help of the aunt, was to find them another maid, so that I could forfeit a month's pay and leave right away.

I went home and told – not everybody, since I did not want the bush telephones humming with, 'What's she up to *now*?' – but just Henry and Fanny, who were pleased. They had worried about me wearing out my youth in service.

I had a bit of money saved up. Small as my wages were, I had never had time to spend them. I went out and bought some clothes to be an author in.

Coming home one winter day with shopping bags, I found Fanny in the drawing room, pouring a whisky for a worn, middle-aged man, who sat in the bottomless armchair with his knees higher than his head, and looked as if he had been crying. It was not unusual to find Fanny with a customer for her willing ear. She was always available for woes, however dreary or repetitive. Her lunch table was a repository for the world's bores. Easy to be nice to people who are appealing and sensitive in their unhappiness. Much harder to go on being nice to the kind of people that Fanny had to lunch.

The man in the chair was in bad trouble. His wife had T.B., and in those days, before penicillin or even the sulpha drugs, fresh cold air was the standard treatment. She was living in a little hut in his Sussex garden, while he struggled with a decrepit old house full of children.

The last of four helpers had just walked out, leaving the back door open, and the children's puppy had run out and been killed on the railway. The house was a long way from the village, and local dailies would not come. Desperate, the man had come up to London to cast himself on the mercy of Universal Aunts. They knew that I had just left the Fishers, but not that I had retired from the profession. He had come straight to 52 without telephoning.

'Will you come?' He sat forward in the bottomless chair, with his knobby hands hanging between his ankles. 'I need help so desperately.'

'I'm terribly sorry.' Book or no book, I probably would not have gone, from his description of the work. 'I've given up doing those sort of jobs.'

His face hit the carpet.

Fanny wrung her hands. 'I'm so sorry,' she grieved. 'Oh, I do wish we could help.' She was almost ready to go herself, though she could hardly boil water, or sub-let Mary Lott. 'Couldn't you ...?' She raised her circumflex eyebrows at me. 'You couldn't – just go for a little while, and do the – you know –' we had agreed not to tell anyone about the book – 'in the evenings?'

'I never entertain,' said the man, not knowing what 'you know' was. 'Your evenings would be free.' He looked up at me like a basset hound.

I got up and started walking about, to get their pressure off me. I knew I had to go.

I would not have been able to do the 'you know' in the evenings, even if I had not been so tired. My hands would have been too cold to hold a pencil. In Sussex, it was too cold to do anything except dive into bed in socks and sweaters and watch the little pile of snow that drifted in past the wad of newspaper that stuffed the missing window pane.

Much later when my book came out, Major Hampden agonized from South Africa: 'Why didn't you tell us how cold you were? We would have done something.' But there was not much they could have done in that old house where draughts nipped along the stone floor like puppies at your ankles, and although there were fireplaces in the bedrooms, they had all been boarded up to keep the wind from coming down the chimney.

Mrs Hampden was twenty years younger than he was, which made it worse that she was the one who was dying. He had sired these five young children quite late in life. Without her to mother them, he was at a loss. He went off every day to some job he had in East Grinstead, while I tried to cope with the beautiful old house, which did not have a door or window that fitted, a tap that did not drip, a drain that ran free. The kitchen stove was a monstrous encrusted relic. No point in cleaning it now. Three of the children went to school on the local bus which stopped at the end of our lane. The other two were at home with me, locked in the daily battle against chilblains, hacking coughs and nappies to be washed in cold water when the copper would not light.

There were no deliveries, and I could not get to the shops because my car would not start, and I could not take the baby and the two-year-old on the dot-and-carry bicycle. Major Hampden brought back for us what he remembered from my list and what he could afford, which was not enough. Medical costs had all but ruined them. Bills nagged like a headache.

The older children would come home from school tired and grumpy, stumbling down the iron ruts of the lane in their cobbled boots, to upset the housebound equilibrium of the little ones and me.

'He's messed up my puzzle. Why did you let him touch my puzzle?'

'We always had jam for tea when Mrs Jellow was here.'

'That's a lie.'

'We had parsnip jam. She made it.'

'You hated it.'

'Mother's hungry. Why hasn't anyone been out to her?'

'She wouldn't eat her lunch.'

'She's *got* to eat it. Dad told you. I'm not going to school tomorrow.'

'Why don't you pick up Ruth when she cries? Mrs Wrigley always did.'

'Mrs Wrigley was an old goat.'

'Wasn't.'

'Was.'

'She hated you.'

By the time the poor Major limped in, having walked three-quarters of a mile from where his car had conked out, everyone was yelling or crying, including me. When I agreed to go to Sussex, I had thought they would be like the family in *Little Women*.

Mrs Hampden, pallid princess in her garden ice house, with her cough that sounded as if it came up a mine shaft, fought all the battles with us in her anxious mind. Perhaps she might have got better if she were not so worried. Isolation and rest were meant to include mental relaxation, but she knew how bad things were for us in the house, and she felt that she was the cause of it.

The children visited her one at a time, and twice a day she came into the house to wash, creeping round the kitchen on sticks of legs that ended in boy's boots, trying to pick things up, or scrape the bottom of a pan, and having to be restrained. All she was allowed to do was mending, and this she did endlessly, her fingers emerging blue from the mittens the oldest girl had knitted.

Lovely to me, she was, and I loved her dearly. I loved all of them, and I might have got sucked into staying, at least until the six-year-old and I had finished replacing all the broken lead in the casements with plasticine.

'Please make Mummy well,' the children asked every night,

inside the bed, not beside it, since they would have frozen where they knelt.

No one answered, and finally the whole family, carrying kittens and broken tennis racquets and corners of old sucked blankets, departed to her parents' home in South Africa, and I went back to London to write my book.

7

How did one write a book?

The first thing was to have something to write with. I bought exercise books and new pencils. Writing is easier when you don't know how difficult it is. I wrote *One Pair of Hands* in three weeks, sitting in the corner of the drawing-room sofa, with people coming in and out, and arguing, and polishing the fire dogs, and having tea, and playing the piano and making jokes.

Michael Joseph had given me only one piece of advice. When I asked him, as we shook hands under the Daphne du Maurier dream picture, 'How do I – I mean, how *do* you write a book?' he had said, 'Don't be afraid. Imagine that something extraordinary has happened to you. You're coming into a roomful of people you know quite well and saying, "Do you *know* what happened to me?" "No, what?" "It was like this." And you tell it.'

'Oh listen,' he said in the narrow hall, opening the front door on to Bloomsbury Street. 'Don't worry about how to write. Just write.'

Nowadays, when people whose friends tell them that they write such good letters and ought to write a book, write me one of their good letters to ask me how it's done, I pass on Michael's advice. Just write.

That may be fairly irritating to them, if they are hoping that I will divulge some magic clue that has kept me in business all these years.

Writing a book felt important. Now when I walked in the Park with Ugly, I imagined that people with friends and mates and prams saw that I had chosen to be alone because I was thinking. Preoccupied, purposeful. They would envy me if they knew I was an author.

My brain, so long unused, was excited by the novelty. At night, it would not turn off. It kept me awake, being excited. I would have to go and be sick in the bathroom, and Fanny would hear me and get up and be excited with me, holding my head over the double basins in the massive wood and marble Victorian washstand, whose cupboards smelled of Glycothymoline and Friar's Balsam.

Henry was very proud. He had always been proud of things I had done, from passing the Brownie sewing test with a blood-stained handkerchief hem to fighting my way up to be captain of the second eleven at cricket, so that I could choose myself to bowl.

He took me to a dinner of the Dickens Fellowship. The President was Compton Mackenzie, whose grandfather had been a friend of Charles Dickens. I had read *Sinister Street* and *Carnival*, and he was impressive to me, as an author, with his amused, questioning face, and spry pointed beard. He was obviously a writer. You knew that. I was just a girl who had written a book. We shared the nickname of Monty. That was all.

Across the table from me, my father leaned towards Compton Mackenzie in the President's chair and said with expansive pride, 'My daughter has written a book.'

I sagged down in my chair to try to reach under the table to kick him, but Monty turned his bright eyes on me and said, 'Splendid. I'd love to see the proofs – if you'd like me to?'

The story I had pencilled into the exercise books was, and still is, expectably naive, and in places rather prejudiced. Monty did not mess about with it, or try to rewrite it. He tidied up a few loose utterances and taught me one enduring lesson, how to write dialect.

Trying to convey cockney, the manuscript was peppered with apostrophes like a fly-specked ceiling. He showed me that it was not the dropping of aitches, but the choice and arrangement of words, the rhythm and the turn of phrase which enable a reader to create an accent in his mind's ear.

He lived in a cottage in the Vale of Health on Hampstead Heath, where he collected girls, in the nicest possible way. Invited to drop in on him any time, I would usually find two or three other young women sitting on the floor drinking coffee and wine and listening to him talk.

I doted on him. He was my sponsor, as my grandfather Henry Fielding Dickens had been his sponsor when he was a Law student of the Inner Temple. Unasked, he offered to write a foreword for *One Pair of Hands*. He wrote, among other fine and helpful things, that the book was not quite as good as *Pickwick Papers*, and I had made a brave start.

Incredibly, with the great good luck that has dogged me all my days, the book was a fair success. With all its faults, it probably got by on a certain spontaneity and youthful enthusiasm that one can never recapture, once experience begins to creep in. It was serialized in the *Sunday Chronicle*, with pictures of me, fat in my pink satin court dress and feathers, and thinner in a work apron, scrubbing the kitchen floor at 52.

Ellen Page could not see the point, since she had washed that lino just last Wednesday. Some of the Dickens aunts were outraged that I had played fast and loose with the name. Just as parents think that sex stopped with their generation, Charles Dickens was expected to be the last family member to appear in print. When the double-page newspaper spread appeared, there were dark rumblings about the Yellow Press.

One of my Runge aunts was miffed for a different reason. She had at the time four maids in her elegant flat in Eaton Square. They had been with her a long time, because she was kind and paid good wages. But my book was dangerous propaganda. She read it quickly, then locked it away, for fear that the maids might take it into the kitchen and become corrupted.

My life was transformed. Suddenly I was an author. I was invited to publishers' parties, and asked to review books and write articles on careers for women and how to cook spaghetti.

One Pair of Hands sold 6,622 copies in the original edition. Minus my £50 advance, my first royalty cheque was £341 19s. 10d.

*

When you have had a certain success with your first book, the second one is even more important. People are watching, to reassure themselves that you are merely a nine days' wonder. Meaning to write something new and different, I bought a second hand typewriter for four pounds in Kilburn, and started on the novel that is everyone's second book, if it was not their first, based on my own childhood and growing up.

Fifty-two was all of a sudden full of bottles and scalded milk and nurses. Because there was no room in her flat above the surgery where Denys performed his fashionable caesarians and hip dysplasia corrections on prize greyhounds, Doady was in my sunny front bedroom with her second baby. I moved into my brother's little room next door, that had been fitted out like a cabin when he was a cadet at Osborne. The baby screamed all the time. There was something wrong with him. That Christmas, which we spent in the country at Cookham Dean, because the war had started and London was expected to be blown up within a few weeks, Doady had him in a basket on the piano. He was navy blue and puny, and people said that she would never rear him. She did.

A lot of people had left town. Rents had dropped. I took a small flat, in Mayfair at last, and finished my novel *Mariana* quickly, before the call-up of women began.

8

Scrap iron was the cry at that time. In those limbo days, when people carried sandwiches and cigarettes in the empty cases of their gas masks, I borrowed a pony and cart from the coster's stable in the Portobello Road and went round the houses in Pembridge Villas and Chepstow Crescent, taking away old pipes and bedsteads to make into guns. As soon as my book was finished, I was going to be a nurse.

Saturated with *A Farewell to Arms*, I joined the Red Cross as a V.A.D., wearing one of those romantic grey-blue uniforms with a white apron and a flowing white veil. Nobody wanted me. London hospitals were no busier yet. A friend of ours who was a doctor got me into a hospital in Windsor for the necessary ward work I needed to complete my training. I went up and down on the train every day, and the other nurses let me sweep the floor and cut the bread and butter and polish the brass taps of the basin where doctors washed their immaculate hands after rounds.

One evening when the ward was a fevered maelstrom of nurses scuttling about with bedpans and tin basins and tooth mugs, I was sitting in a corner of the kitchen, because I was afraid to go into the ward unless I was invited.

'What are you doing, sitting here idle?' Assistant Matron, who went everywhere as if it were a hundred yard dash, darted into the kitchen and turned down the gas under the kettle, which was on the boil permanently, night and day.

'They won't give me anything to do.'

'Come and talk to Matron,' Ass. Mat. said. 'If you want to be a nurse, you may as well do it right.'

Matron was an attractive woman in her late forties, with

greying sausage curls and a manner at once bustling and refined. I was terrified of her, not because she was a terrifying woman, but because she was the Matron. Out of uniform, I might have found her easy. I daresay even Miss Strudwick, met outside St Paul's, might have been quite old shoe.

My chat in Matron's office was the last time I was in there, except for sins and crimes. She agreed to take me for training, and I left Chepstow Villas and started as a probationer nurse at King Edward VII Hospital. I found some stables in a mews at the edge of Windsor Park, behind the nurses' home, where I left Tonia my horse and Ugly my dog. I could take them out when I had time or energy, which was not often.

I had worked hard as a cook-general, but that was nothing compared to being a probationer in the strict nursing school of a busy hospital. I was afraid some of the time, hungry most of the time, and tired all the time. In the lecture room, I sat in the back row, so that I could fall asleep behind the broad back of the nurse from Cumberland while Sister Tutor talked. But just as I had recognized a spiritual home when I first went down to a kitchen as a worker, not a visitor, I recognized as mine the cloistered, esoteric world of hospital.

It was my first experience of the quick, needy friendships that come from a fellowship of situation and purpose.

I had never had a friend like Joan, who was my senior on night duty on Queen Mary ward. We ran the place better than the day staff. We prized our independence. The gastrics and emphysemas and worn out old ladies belonged to us. In the daytime, in bed, or riding in the park, or in the teashops that still had cakes, I looked forward to eight-thirty, when Joan and I took over our little world.

For the first few hours the work never stopped. But late at night, when most of the patients were asleep or quiescent and had stopped calling on God or the bedpan, Joan and I would waltz down one side of that long expanse of floor, which the derelict ward maid polished every day with a brick wrapped in a cloth, and up the other side, while the exhausted young house surgeon wrote up his notes under the shaded desk lamp, and would not dance with us.

I had never had a friend like Kay, who could turn a saving joke out of any disaster. The sister of Men's Medical, who had pin tucks in her apron bib and a cap like a vanilla soufflé, told her, 'You are too crude to make a nurse, Nurse.' The men did not mind being asked, 'Have you shat?' instead of, 'Have you had your bowels open?' At night, Kay used to climb in over the balcony with fish and chips and meat pies for the starving guardsman patients from Windsor barracks across the road.

I had never had friends like some of the patients, never experienced that kind of intense, brief intimacy. For a time, you are closer to them than anyone in their world. When they leave, claimed by their families, looking strange in their clothes, you may never see them again.

In 1940, a nurse was a cross between a nun and a slave, and a probationer was as low as the bedwheels off which on slow afternoons we scraped the built-up wax with a kitchen knife.

Things had not changed much since Florence Nightingale elevated the status of the profession. We still had three pleats, as she had, round the skirts of our long blue dresses, in which you had to kneel on the floor in front of Home Sister to make sure you had not secretly shortened the hem. We wore what was called the Dorothy cap, an impractical affair which returned from the laundry in a stiff half circle. You had to stitch and gather the curved side into a cap with a turned back brim, fastened to your head with iron grips. Some people made beautiful pleated caps. I never could, but cigarettes and sweets were in short supply and you could usually bribe someone deft to sew your cap. We wore high studded collars, which shrank in the wash and choked you, and pinched the remains of my double chin. When you lose as much fat as I had, the extra skin is still there. In the cake shops and cinemas and bars of the town, you could always tell a nurse from King Edward VII by the red mark round her neck like a suicidal scar.

We wore black stockings and shoes, white aprons with starched belts, and long sleeves with removable stiff cuffs like little flower pots. The etiquette of the cuffs took a probationer at least a week to learn.

You went to breakfast with your sleeves down and your cuffs on, and when you came into the ward, you took off your cuffs and parked them somewhere and rolled up your sleeves to start work. When Sister had finished castigating the night nurses for sins real and imaginary, you rolled down your sleeves, put on your cuffs and gathered round the desk to hear the senior night nurse, now quivering with indignation and nervous exhaustion, read the night report. When that was over and you could at last answer the increasingly desperate cries of Miss Newington at the end of the ward for 'that thing', you took off your cuffs and rolled up your sleeves again until the next formal occasion.

Once when my doctor friend came into the ward, I made the mistake of saying 'Hullo'. Sister's horror was not only that I actually knew a doctor – 'You mean, Nurse, that you actually know him *socially*?' – but that I had spoken to him without my cuffs.

Like the Roman Church in Italy, which used not to allow women in churches in sleeveless dresses, King Edward VII forbade you to leave the ward with bare forearms. Once a patient was having a terrible nosebleed. We tried everything. We sat him up. We laid him down. We pressed every pressure point above the waist. Still he bled, all over the counterpane, which was not due to be changed until tomorrow. It seemed that he would soon pass out from loss of blood. One of the house surgeons came running from Casualty.

'Ice,' he said over his shoulder.

We had no refrigerator on the ward. Sister jerked her head at me and I ran out of the ward, thrilled to be sent on a life or death mission, along the green corridor, down a flight of stairs, along another corridor to the stairs that led to the kitchens.

A grip on my arm like a gin trap jerked me to a stop. Assistant Matron's eyes were blazing.

'Where are you going, Nurse?'

'To the kitchen . . . get ice . . . this man . . . bleed to death . . .'

'Where are your cuffs?'

'It's an emergency. I told you, this man –'

'You never leave the ward without your cuffs, Nurse.'

With Ass. Mat. watching, I had to walk back, run when I was round the corner, find my cuffs, roll down my sleeves and put on the cuffs as I ran down to the kitchen. One of the vegetable peelers was a friend of mine. He had been on the ward with a hernia.

'Give me a bowl of ice, Sharkie.'

'She'll play war with me.' He looked at the back of the vegetable cook. 'Have to ask her.' Evidently the etiquette in the kitchen was as bad as on the ward.

I gabbled my tale about blood and ice, and the cook took her big arms out of the bowl of vegetables from which she was soaking the flavour for tomorrow's lunch, and trod with slow ceremony to the refrigerator. By the time I panted back to the ward, the man had fainted, but the bleeding had stopped anyway, and I had my cuffs on.

Of all the staff at the hospital, Sister Bolger on Men's Surgical was the one I feared the most. But I learned a lot from her. She was a terrible tartar of a woman, but she was a marvellous nurse. Nobody could get away with anything. A terminal patient could not even get away with dying, if Sister Bolger had decided that he would live. She had no life outside the hospital. She would stay on the ward hour after hour, all night if necessary, to nurse a very sick man, not only with her enormous skill and experience, but with the power of her iron will.

Tall and man-shaped, with heavy teeth and loping strides, she treated us like galley slaves. We grumbled and hated her, and yet we sensed a curious version of love in her wanting each one of us to be as good a nurse as she was. She did not like probationers, but because of the war, they were training more nurses, and every ward had at least two of us.

I was her special victim. Anything that happened had to be my fault.

'Na-a-as Diggins!' I can hear that Lancastrian voice now, ringing down the ward, as she discovered a broken thermometer, or a thrombotic patient without his knee pillow. When I first came to the ward, she used to bellow, 'Who has done this?'

As she got to know me, it was shortened to, 'Na-a-as Diggins!'
She would wipe the floor with you in front of the whole ward.
The patients used to give me sweets afterwards, like a child with
a hurt finger.

In the days before antibiotics, the risk of infection was much
greater. Patients still quite often died of things like blood
poisoning and pneumonia. The quality of the nursing was vital.
There must be some men who are only alive today because of
Sister Bolger.

Towards the end of my three months on her ward, there was
an explosion in a chemical factory near us. Several men were
brought in, very badly burned. Sister did not seem to leave the
ward for about four days, except to change her apron. Her raw-
boned masculine face became gaunter, the eyes deep in their
grey sockets. She fought for those burn cases almost as if – the
thought came to me when I saw her strained face as she irrigated
a man's shoulder yet one more time – as if she were giving birth
to the new life his body needed. But when he died, and his
family came creeping to the door of the ward, diminished by
tragedy and the intimidating strangeness of the hospital, she
would not even speak to them.

'Give them his clothes,' she told me. That was all. They were
not her patients. Her humanity was at once boundless and
limited.

After Men's Surgical, I was sent to the private wards, known
as 'going on Privates'. The work was not so hard as on the big
open wards, because there were fewer patients, and some of
them were there not because they were ill enough to be in the
hospital, but rich enough to pay for it. I had to resurrect the
Dixon voice for some of them, because they treated the nurses
like servants.

Most of them treated us like friends, or their children. Mrs
Dewar, all lavender water and ribbons after the first disgusting
days of her cholecystectomy. The old man with the amputated
toes and the endless supply of black market chocolates. Dora
who had lost her baby just after she heard she had lost her pilot

husband. Curtis Brown, the literary agent, who used to have books brought in for me. It was good to have more time to talk to patients. In the ward, five minutes chat leaning on a broom, or resting a tray on the hip, and it would be, 'Na-a-as Diggins!'

It was also restful not to have to scuttle down the ward with five loaded bedpans on top of each other in order to get the round done on time. Bedpan rounds in a ward without curtains between the beds was one of the most successful devices for keeping the ward patients humiliated. Also constipated. The money spent on enema soap alone could have been saved to buy more wheeled screens.

When I started as a probationer, I thought I had given up writing and would be a nurse for ever. I might be at King Edward VII still, just about retiring now as Matron, beloved and feared by all. But the chance to draw breath on Privates made room also for the stirrings of the writer's guilt that has always dogged me, along with the luck. When *Mariana* was published, I had bought a new typewriter, as well as the first refrigerator ever seen at 52, a tiny affair with two ice trays beaten into grotesque shapes by Henry trying to get the ice out. On one of my days off, I fetched the typewriter from London and started to write about being a nurse.

After I caught chickenpox from a patient with shingles, I had been moved to a single room, and Home Sister had forgotten to move me back to sharing. I wrote every evening in my room after supper, instead of studying for my Preliminary exams. As if they knew, it was announced at breakfast, along with the other knells, that I was to go on night duty. So I wrote every morning in bed, putting the papers under the covers and the typewriter under the bed when Home Sister came round at noon to wake up the night staff to make sure they were asleep.

Some of the nurses would sneak out after she had been round. I used to sneak the typewriter out again and keep myself awake stuffing digestive biscuits, wrongly named, because if you eat enough of them you get sick. Not the excited throwing up that

Fanny and I shared over the Victorian marble. Being a writer was not intoxicating any more. It was part of the pattern of life.

'Seven o'clock, Nurse!'

The evening thump on the door was like a clod of earth on a coffin lid. Some of the day staff were coming off duty, relaxed and chattering, while the night nurses, grim and silent, pinned and studded themselves into clean uniforms with fingers numb from too little sleep. In the dining room, day nurses were having supper while we breakfasted at the other end of the room off cold scrambled eggs and sodden toast, left over from what they had had that morning. When you came off duty at eight the next day, you would get the supper they were having now.

Once at 8.30 a.m., I was still laying out the body of a woman who had escaped us in the night. The day staff should be doing it, but the unwritten rule was, 'You let them die, you lay them out.'

Ass. Mat. telephoned the ward to summon me to supper.

'Tell her I'm laying out a body.'

'She says to come to the dining room *now* and go back and finish your work after.'

I had to put down the tow I was stuffing into the woman's anus and go up to a supper of baked sheep's hearts and macaroni.

Henry wrote a letter to the *Daily Telegraph*, complaining that in a time of national crisis, the nurses the country so badly needed were being brutalized by being forced to eat baked sheep's hearts in the middle of laying out a body. The *Telegraph* printed it, but the system did not change.

The only thing that happened was that Mrs Mulholland on Gynae saw a magazine story I had written last year, and showed it to Matron. She thought Matron would be so pleased. She wasn't. She told me with some pride that she had recently refused permission for a theatre nurse to play the piano at a concert. She was not going to have any of her nurses making a spectacle of herself in public, much less a probationer who had come to her office in a dirty apron.

This was worse than the aunts and the Yellow Press. The Ministry of Labour still allowed you to move from job to job, as long as it was war work. If I was going to finish *One Pair of Feet*, I had better get out while I could.

9

I sent Tonia to live with Doady, who had moved with her children to a farm near Maidenhead when Denys went into the Army. Ugly stayed on with the man at the mews stables. They had grown fond of each other, and it seemed kinder to leave him there on the edge of the Great Park than to drag him back to London, where the Blitz was on, and I was going to work in a factory.

I went to a training school in Perivale to learn to be a fitter. We learned about the gravity of metals and how to make male and female squares. One had to fit precisely into the other. We spent hours filing these things by hand and testing them with a micrometer and throwing them away because we had filed too much. It took me about a week to produce one passable set, and even then you could, as the instructor said, drive a bus through the join. I had thought there would be machines to do this kind of job. If the war effort depended on my filing male and female squares, it was a poor outlook.

Through a Kensington friend, I got myself a job in the inspection department at Sunbeam Talbot, up near Little Wormwood Scrubs and the railway sheds. They were repairing Rolls-Royce Spitfire engines for fighter planes, which had failed on test, or been damaged in a crash.

The engines were broken down and washed in giant oily tubs in the dismantling section, where a man named Fred used to pocket every tenth carburettor tube to make into a cigarette lighter. The pieces were then brought in on a cart and spread on benches in the big inspection shop where we worked in teams, eight to an engine. You were taught your own bit, and you worked on that, engine after engine, unless you were ambitious and wanted to learn another section. I learned all the sections, to stave off boredom. Some people stayed on the valves or the oil pipes or the cam rockers for the duration of the war.

Once the management, sensing the boredom, offered lectures on the internal combustion engine, hoping that it would improve morale if we knew where our bit fitted and how it worked. Only a few people went to any of the lectures.

'I know what I'm doing. I don't want to be bothered with that other stuff in my lunch hour,' most people said, like the woman in Lyons Corner House, where I had once worked briefly in the kitchen, who did nothing but wash out metal teapots over a jet of water like a bedpan washer.

When I asked her how she could stand it, she said, 'Well, I been doing this job for twenty years. I know the work, see?'

I started on the valves and moved up through piston rings and oil pump and cams to the carburettor and supercharger, and the reduction gear, which converted the speed of the engine to what was needed for the propeller. The supercharger was known as the Blower, and sometimes it was blocked up with bits of dead seagulls which had been sucked in.

You wrote a report on every piece you inspected, down to the tiniest screw, and Mr Sid Whiffen and George, in brown coats like ironmongers, ordered the parts from our reports. When it was one of Fred's tenth engines, you did not leave the bench to go across the wind-blasted yard to the dismantling shop and say, 'Look here, Fred, it's not right to steal bits off fighter planes during the Battle of Britain.' You wrote, 'Supply 1 carb tube', and George or Sid Whiffen filled in the parts number.

It was not a taxing job, and the gossip and jokes round the inspection bench almost made up for the monotony. Sid Whiffen and George and the foremen in charge of the various teams of women were old factory hands. They were driven stoically crazy by the motley assortment of violinists, housewives, cripples, grandmothers and amateur whores whom it was their fate to oversee, strictly enough for aircraft safety, but leniently enough to keep them on the job. On our bench, there was nobody who had ever worked in a factory before except old Gwen, who had been in munitions in the First War and still had yellow fingernails.

Our foreman was Frank. He was quite proper, and the women used to tease him. He hated what he called a dirty mouth, which amused Jean, who had one. She was the traditional heart-of-gold witty bawd, who would be at home anywhere in history or literature. She was one of the new friends the war brought me, rakish, insolent, pushy from the bottom up, instead of from the top down, like people I used to know in the old debby world. Frank, who was respectably married, was half afraid of Jean, but half delighted. Her tarty teasing made him feel shockingly male.

Factory life, like hospital life, did not seem to have much to do with the war. In the relentless monotony of the work, any sense of purpose gradually dwindled in focus down to the weekly pay packet.

From the time the tea cart hove into view at nine a.m. and you held your mug under the urn tap – an enormous mug, since any size was filled for a penny – to the knocking off bell at five-thirty, the day was a contest to steal a few minutes off without getting caught. Taking a mike, it was called. You could go looking for information from the men in Parts. You could take a scratched finger to First Aid. You could suspect a hairline crack in a pump casing and take five minutes mike in the next shop with the jolly men who tested cylinder blocks with sprayed chalk.

We complained about everything, from Mr Whiffen's natural desire for speed, since the planes were needed back in the air, to the lack of towels in the ladies' room. When the management, anxious to keep us, although they probably would not have employed any of us in peace time, put in a hot air blower, the women used to take a fifteen minute mike to wash their hair and dry it, kneeling under the blower, where Frank could not come in after them.

I worked in the factory for about a year. Every morning when I rode my bicycle through the mean grey North Kensington streets, past the Tennis Club, now violated by vegetables, and up St Quintin Avenue against a head wind, I knew that I could not stand it much longer. Every winter Monday when I parked the bike in the rack, stepped through the little door in the huge door of the vast, freezing shop where the heat had been turned off all weekend and picked up a frosted gear wheel, I vowed it was the last week that I would work for Sunbeam Talbot.

When I came home through a foggy dusk to thaw out in front of the fire, a dreadful stench was drawn out of clothes and skin by the heat. I smelled like the engine room of a tanker. I could never get free of it, no matter how many hot baths I took with the aid of the little gas geyser I had bought with my *One Pair of Hands* advance. I was too tired to write in the evenings, so I finished *One Pair of Feet* at weekends when Henry and Fanny went to the country. I grew more restless through a tantalizing spring and an oil-vapoured summer when the gear wheels were lubricated with sweat and your forehead grew black from wiping it with the back of your hand.

The money was good, but my heart was not in it. I began to make mistakes, and was hauled up by Sid Whiffen for not calling for Mod 23 D on the valve seating. He knew this modification had to go on every valve of this type that came through. He could have corrected the report himself, but that was not the way it worked. He was a stickler, like Sister Bolger, and though we mocked him at the time, he probably kept that whole section going, and it was due to people like him that there were planes for pilots to fly.

Doady was immured in the country with four small children and Nanny Brown, two bicycles and no car. I had the idea that Tonia was harness-broken and had been driven by her former owner. At the back of the dusty barn, there was a little governess cart like a brown tub with a door at the back, and I found a set of driving harness at the top end of the Portobello Road, where the costers kept ponies.

We hooked up the lively little bay mare. She pulled the cart quite docilely round the lanes for an hour, so I agreed to the children's clamour to be taken for a drive.

Tonia's docility had been merely a chance. Trotting serenely down one of those straight, narrow roads the Romans left behind, something happened. I will never know what it was, since all memory was blotted out from me and Nanny Brown, and the children were too small and shaken to understand. After a blackout of what may have been ten minutes or two hours, I woke to find myself sitting at the side of that stony Roman road with Nanny's bloody head in my lap, the wrecked cart in the ditch on the other side of the road, and no sign of horse or children.

They had been picked up by a passing motorist, who telephoned for an ambulance. Tonia was found that night with a wild eye and bits of broken harness and cart shaft dangling from her.

Nanny Brown, turning to shield the baby from the mare, who was kicking the cart to bits, had got a hoof in the head. She was in King Edward VII Hospital for weeks. Ridden with guilt, I had to go and see her.

One Pair of Feet had been published, and I had an idea what the hospital thought about it. I had to wear dark glasses anyway, over the bloodshot eye that sloshed about in the side of a face that still looked like a squashed tomato. In a wide hat and turned up collar, I went in at the unfamiliar front entrance. The nurses always went in and out at the side, by the path to the nurses' home. I saw two of them hurrying off duty with that toes-out rocking waddle you get from going up and down a ward too many times.

The porter did not recognize me as I went through the hall towards the stairs. Oh God, the smell of carbolic and ether! I could hardly stand it. Even the antiseptic curved corner between wall and floor struck home with a pang. I was sick with envy of the staff in the busy corridors, the porters with trolleys, the doctors with flapping white jackets, the nurses who looked at me as either invisible or a nuisance, as I had done on visiting days when the hospital was over-run with apologetic strangers.

Although I had bashed confidently so many times through the swing doors of Women's Surgical, I felt nervous going into the ward, trying to see which bed Nanny was in without being spotted by Sister, making up charts at her desk.

Nurse Robinson – with a white belt now, how did she ever pass her Prelim? – came up to take the flowers I had brought.

'Dickens!' Her eyes widened. 'What on earth have you done to your face?'

'I was in the same accident as Miss Brown.' I was dismayed to realize I did not know Nanny's first name.

'Listen, kid.' Robinson spoke behind her hand in the dinky way she used to pass on bits of hospital gossip. 'Don't let anyone see you. You know that book?'

'What book?'

'The one you wrote. They played war about it. Your name is mud. Hutch was caught reading it, and Matron called a special meeting and told her off in front of everybody.'

'Why?'

'Well, listen. You know what they're like. They thought you laughed at them.'

'Nurse Robinson!' The staff nurse called from the door of the sluice, where old Rob was probably supposed to be cleaning test tubes and sputum mugs. Nanny Brown groaned and sighed and fell asleep. I sat by the bed with my shoulders hunched and my head hanging until Sister was trapped by a demanding relation in a corner of the ward, and I could escape.

Years afterwards, I heard from a nurse at King Edward VII that they collected all the probationers together at the beginning of their training and asked them, 'Have any of you people read Charles Dickens?'

'Oh yes.' Hands up eagerly, believing in those early days that it is possible to curry favour.

'Very good.' Leading them on. 'Have any of you people read any books by Monica Dickens?'

Well, they did all right on the first question. Some hands go up again. A hopeful voice at the back has read *One Pair of Feet*.

The axe descends. 'If any of you people are ever found reading those rubbishy lies . . .'

One Pair of Feet was not subversive. It was the truth, with a few changes to satisfy the laws of conscience or libel. The reaction of the nursing world seems surprising now, when so many changes have been made, and the puritan discipline of places like King Edward VII seems as remote as Sairey Gamp.

Nursing newspapers were scandalized, mostly on the grounds that the book was *funny*.

'Miss Dickens is not acquainted with the sane and wholesomely humoured women and girls who do their work with balanced minds and intelligence.'

In a review of the book, the *Nursing Times* said:

'If you take it seriously – and not as an essay in facetiousness – it gives an unpleasant picture of hospital life. Miss Dickens ... appears to have intelligence ... yet she chooses the hospital for her professional training because a doctor who had been a house surgeon there told her that the bath water was always hot. What a way to set about a professional training!'

'... It is a queer age that we live in in many ways, but surely it is more than strange that a person who has had, one supposes, a fair education and home training, will tell a lie to save herself a little trouble – merely the trouble of putting on a clean apron – and apparently think it clever and report it to the world at large.'

A Letter to the Editor from an S.R.N. pointed out that either the book was fiction, and therefore lies, or the hospital should immediately be 'struck off the lists of approved training centres.'

The book was made into a film, with Rosamund John as the nurse and a newcomer, Stewart Granger, with his pyjama jacket open to show bristly black chest hairs. It was called *The Lamp Still Burns*, because *One Pair of Feet* was considered bad propaganda for nursing. They used nothing from the book except a brief bit of dialogue with a gastric patient with whom Kay and I used to joke on Men's Medical.

Returning to the hospital at Windsor had been wildly nostalgic. Taking Ugly back to his mews home after a walk in the Park – he was just as pleased to get back to his new friend as he had been to see me – I stopped by the gate that led through the garden to the nurses' home, and looked up at the window where Joan and I used to sit on the wide sill and wonder what we were doing shut up in this nunnery. I used to puzzle over how people like Sister Bolger and Ass. Mat. could stay in the same institution for years and years and see nothing of the world. But I was beginning to understand that the pull of belonging can sometimes be stronger than the pull of independence.

A friend was in a London hospital, and I went to see her. She was in a single room off the ward, since she had had a thyroidectomy, which needs peace and quiet. She seemed a bit neglected. I tidied up the bed and brought her a bedpan when nobody answered her bell. The nurse who finally came breathlessly in was grateful, not resentful.

'Are you short of nurses?' I asked.

'Terribly. A lot of people have gone into the Services. There aren't enough new ones coming in.'

She was a tall fair girl, broad-shouldered and big-footed like me. As she stood against the light from the window, I hazed my eyes out of focus to see myself inside her stiff dress and square-bibbed apron. I wanted to be a nurse again. I had never really stopped being one.

No one would have me. Although it was 1942 and there was an increasing drain on people available for jobs at home, the big London hospitals turned me down.

The hierarchy, like the *Nursing Times*, had been affronted that a nurse should make jokes about such sacred structures as protocol and cuffs and probationers being lower than the bed wheels. If those bulwarks should be stripped away, and the nurses turn like ungrateful worms, what would be left of their life's work? The patients? To some of the nursing bureaucracy, a necessary evil, at best. Mitred counterpane corners and fractured femurs with their suspension beams all in line when Matron came round and no twopenny magazines on the bed lockers – ah, there was the glory.

In hospital after hospital, a promising interview would end with a second look at my name on the application form, and a sharp upward glance.

'Aren't you the nurse who . . .'

I tried a false name, but identity cards and insurance papers soon betrayed that. It made it worse, at the Hammersmith Hospital in Du Cane Road, that I was not only a subversive nurse, but a dishonest one, just as the *Nursing Times* had said.

I was still at Sunbeam Talbot. You could not switch war work until you had another job. That was it then. If the nursing profession did not want me, I would stay on the shop floor and become a female Sid Whiffen, training batch after batch of silly women until I retired, with a tea party in the canteen, a silver cigarette box from the management and a burnished carburettor tube lighter from Fred in Dismantling.

My morale was somewhat dismantled, like everybody else's at that stage of the war. Churchill, persuasive with after-dinner port on the nine o'clock news, was an oasis in long stretches of boredom and acceptance in which many people talked less about the war news than whether the jam ration was going up or down. War, like depression or bereavement, makes you feel it will go on for ever.

At the end of 1942, we said, 'It will always be like this.' We sewed strips of different fabric round the bottom of our coats to satisfy the sadism of fashion designers who had somehow been allowed to launch a Longer Look in the middle of wartime clothes rationing. We ate Spam and whalemeat and carrot pie, and learned so steadfastly to stand in queues that we have never forgotten it.

Even air raids were not dramatic any more, but a feature of daily life. Henry, who was an air raid warden in a Churchill siren suit and a First War tin hat, had built a home air raid shelter in the back yard of 52, where the Sunday cricketers had called to each other, 'Steady the Buffs,' and, 'Good shot, sir!' It was a small square bunker like a septic tank, about five feet underground and two above, with two bunks on either side and a tiny space between.

Air raids started at dusk. Most people had dinner early and then went to ground. Henry continued to have his dinner at eight o'clock, brought out to the shelter by Minnie, if the warning siren had sounded. Squadrons of bombers droned over Kensington. The anti-aircraft guns barked in the Park. An oil bomb landed – whomf – in the garden next door, but Henry went back and forth in his tin hat to fetch his claret and the North Kensington Lawn Tennis Club port decanter and the bowl of walnuts. On Fanny's birthday, he wore a dinner jacket.

I slept with them in the shelter, getting up at dawn when the All Clear sounded to snatch an hour or two in bed before it was time to drag on my overalls and bicycle to the factory. The oil bomb was the closest shave we had, but there was the talisman feeling that because we had the shelter, the Germans would aim elsewhere.

Hatred of the Germans had dulled to a nagging dislike, and Hitler had been reduced to a feeble comic figure in songs like 'Run Adolf, run, Adolf, run, run, run'.

10

Into this stagnant pond of tired acceptance came a letter.

It was from the Sister Tutor of the Homoeopathic Hospital (it was spelt with three o's then) in Queen Square, Bloomsbury. She had liked my book. She knew, she said, that it had upset some in the profession, but if only I had been a nurse at her hospital, I would have a different tale to tell.

I read the letter again during the morning break, with my vast grubby mug of tea at my elbow, and the blower spread out in unwieldy parts all round. When the bell went to start work, I took a five minute mike to the public telephone.

That afternoon, I got Sid Whiffen's permission to leave early, went home to scrub, and took the Tube to Russell Square to be interviewed by Sister Tutor and Matron, an intimidating flat woman of the Miss Strudwick variety, who would have looked equally suitable as a man. They were willing to take me. Since I had passed no State exams, the experience at King Edward VII counted for nothing, and I would have to start all over again at the bottom as a bed wheel probationer.

Life looked up. I could ask for my cards at the factory tomorrow. Even the war might end some day.

In Notting Hill Gate station, people were already coming down with blankets and pillows, staking out claims to the painted rectangles on the platform that were their beds night after night during the raids. I travelled up in the filthy old lift and ran down Kensington Park Road to interrupt Fanny giving South African sherry to a woman whose husband had left her for a WAAF, to say I was a nurse again.

Once I started to work at the Homoeopathic Hospital, I understood why I had received that letter from Sister Tutor, known as Toots. It was not that I was desirable, it was that they were so short of nurses they would take even me.

The nurses' home in Great Ormond Street opposite the hospital had been bombed out. We lived in tall buildings that had once been an ant hill of tiny flats and bed-sitting rooms, a short walk away through Queen Square and down an alley where you ran with your cape wrapped round you, coming back after dark on winter evenings. The rooms were doubles and triples, but I was given a room by myself under the roof. I thought it was because Toots, connoisseur of literature, wanted me to be able to write. I found out that it was to keep me away from the other nurses.

For quite a while, nobody spoke to me. Until I got my black and white striped dresses, I wore the blue Windsor uniform dress. When nurses saw me coming, they stepped aside to walk on the other side of the corridor or stairs. At meals, there was often an empty chair next to me.

'Why do they hate me?' I asked a friendly nurse on my ward, whose nature did not include the ingredients of hate.

'We've been warned,' Irene said, 'that you're a dangerous influence. Anybody caught talking to you is going to get shot.'

Toots – oh, that rat. But she went on being nice and jokey with me, and giving me special coaching to win the gynaecology prize tea set. To accept me and reject me at the same time must have been Matron's way of giving Toots her head, and then jerking the rein.

The ban wore off after a while. Matron and Toots had other fish to fry. But for a while I had tasted the poisoned isolation that drives people to think of suicide. Then one of the staff nurses, who wanted my attic room, complained that I was Toots's favourite. I was moved two floors down to share a room with an outraged girl who kept her cases permanently packed so that she could leave at a moment's notice, which left more room for me in drawers and wardrobe.

One of the things she was outraged about was me using the typewriter in bed. There was no sitting room in the nurses' home, or any quiet corners. I used to lug my typewriter back to the hospital after supper and put it on the emergency operating table in the basement and sit on the anaesthetist's stool and try to write bits of a novel about a foreman in an aircraft factory before I was disturbed.

Hitler was a personal nuisance to me, because I had to move my typewriter if there was an air raid and they had to do emergency operations downstairs.

In true homeopathy, you don't do many operations. It runs on the principle of vaccination, that a very tiny dose of what ails you or what you don't want to ail you will stimulate your body to make antibodies, and so you will cure or protect yourself. *Simila similibus curantur.*

To most of the wartime nurses, homeopathy was mysterious witchcraft. There was not time for us to be thoroughly instructed in the purpose of the harmless-looking little pills we were told to give, and so sometimes we either did not give them, or gave them wrong.

Because of the war, the hospital had changed from being specialized to doing general work. There was a normal amount of surgery, and most of the staff were not homeopaths. Some of them still were, however, and this led to some confusion of treatments. One patient coming in with a lump on her breast would have a biopsy and perhaps an immediate mastectomy. Another, with a homeopathic doctor, might choose to try the little pills until the cancer had spread and the mastectomy had to be radical.

I remember an American soldier brought in during an air raid with a mild leg injury, screaming the ward down – 'Gimme morphine!' – when he was approached by Nurse Mann with two of the little white sugar of milk pills we tried on people first to see if they were hypochondriacs.

There were a lot of placebos given, often successfully.

'Oh nurse, the pain, the pain, the drug, I must have the drug' might get an injection of sterile water. 'A-a-ah, oh, the relief, the blessed drug, bless you, nurse, I'll go to slee . . . to slee . . .'

I did not know anything about homeopathy when I went to that hospital. I still don't know much, even after two and a half years there. I saw wonderful results in the skin clinic with some of the natural herb and plant ointments, and many gastric problems cured by diet plus pills. I liked seeing the body cure itself, when it could. But I can still see that man with pneumonia on the ground floor ward. He was an author, a man as likeable as the books he wrote about the English countryside. The sulphonamides were being used effectively against pneumonia, but the patient and his doctor, a disciple of the famous homeopath who treated King George V, persevered with minute doses of the pneumococcus. Much too late they agreed, under pressure, to try sulphadiazine. He was dying anyway, so of course the dear man died, and his doctor said, 'There you are, you see, the sulpha drugs don't work.'

When all else failed, there was always prayer.

In the operating theatre, after the surgeon has put his scrubbed hands into the sterilized gloves, he holds them together to keep them from infection. Mr Tucker, a surgeon who belonged to a holy sect, held them together because he was praying.

He always prayed before an operation, and sometimes during it. If things got tricky, he would take a two minute mike in a corner of the theatre with his head bowed, while his assistant and the scrub nurse hung on to the retractors and artery forceps.

Homeopathic pharmacology, being so neat and portable, was much in favour among missionaries of this same sect. The hospital was, among other things, a school for missionary medical and nursing students.

'Are you saved?' Nurse Anderson used to carol from bed to bed. 'Are you saved?'

'Well, it was a good thing they stuck them tubes up me whatsis before I burst, I'll tell you that,' said old Daddy Newell.

He was one of the bladder daddies on the surgical ward where I first worked, a place of tubes and bottles, constantly awash with urine. Because of the age at which most men yield to a prostatectomy, a lot of the bladder daddies were a bit senile. Short of tying them down, it was impossible to get through to them that they were supposed to stay in bed. It was a frequent sight to see a bladder daddy in his short hospital gown, being pursued by a probationer down a corridor with his tubes and bottles dangling round his skinny bare legs.

The Homoeopathic Hospital was also a general nursing school, and a very good one. Toots was a red-hot instructor, much better than the more domesticated Toots at King Edward VII. Training on the wards was expert and tough, and tougher still because of the war, when there were fewer nurses in civilian hospitals. Responsibility came quicker. You might suddenly find yourself in charge of a small quiet ward at night, when it seemed only yesterday that you were the junior probationer, dashing about all night with urinals and fomentation bowls.

Although there was a constant downgrading of the nurses to keep us in our place, there was also a certain upgrading, because so much was expected of us. Homeo nurses were known to be the best. At Windsor I had learned to work hard, but at the Homeo, I learned commitment, and that nursing is more than technique and muscle and endless endurance. The nun-slave syndrome still applied, but with an element of protectiveness. When Matron watched from her window to see who came in late, or went out without gloves or with coats over uniforms, heading for the Russbar, and what undesirable men waited by the corner lamp post, it was not only because you were a subordinate nurse. It was because you were *her* nurse.

Some of us had been moved into rooms in the Hospital for Nervous Diseases which joined the back of the Homoeopathic. It was evacuated and kept locked, and you went in and out through the door of our hospital, under Matron's window. Before long, we discovered a route out of a top hospital window, along a ledge, over the glass mortuary roof and the slopes of the Nervous Diseases roofs to the far end of Queen Square, where the men waited under a different lamp post.

Matron was pleased that more nurses were staying in their rooms studying, instead of going out at night.

Because I was there longer, the friendships at the Homoeo were even more intense than at King Edward. Many of the nurses lived far away from London and could not get home. If one of my friends had a day or night off with me, we would hare back to 52 to be fed with Minnie's sausages, eaten from the wooden sponge tray across the bath which we shared to save hot water. The little geyser added a boiling trickle, and Fanny sat on a cork-topped stool and listened to our tales of hardship and pathological phenomena.

Fanny was the only person in the family who would still listen. I had bored everyone when I was a servant with my one-track petty stories of life below stairs. The tales of a nurse shut up in a hospital all day and night were even more esoterically dull to those who were not part of that world.

Off duty at the Homoeo, we seldom talked about anything but the patients or the doctors or the nursing staff. I was still writing book reviews for the *Sunday Chronicle*, but it was increasingly difficult to pay attention to reading the books, or writing about them. I was always late with my copy, bicycling down Gray's Inn Road to the office, hoping I would not see anyone I knew there if I was wearing my bluebottle mac and the round blue midwife's cap with the sides turned up like a trapper's.

When I went out to dinner or to a party, it was hard to make normal conversation, even if I stayed awake. People learned not to ask me, 'What do you do?' because I was liable to tell them.

Naturally, when I started another novel, it was about a hospital like the Homoeopathic. It was hard to get into the book. Exams were imminent, and every evening we studied bones and muscles for Anatomy, and sewer systems for Public Health. The nights got shorter, unless you were on night duty. Hospital food got worse and worse. The weekly two-ounce butter and sugar rations seemed to get smaller. The Homoeo's version of a dried egg omelette was fit for nothing but to sole your shoes with.

Exams came, and three Matrons arrived from other hospitals to conduct the oral grilling, and to watch us bandage joints and prepare a post-op bed and lay up a rectal tray. They knew us by numbers only, not names. Toots told me afterwards that at lunch they had started to carry on about *One Pair of Feet*, and how that girl who wrote it must have been a hopeless nurse.

'You've just passed her for her Prelim,' Toots wanted to say. 'You praised her kaolin poultice.'

When I had a week off I went to stay with my sister-in-law, who had evacuated herself and her little boy to a cottage at Bolt Head in Devon. She let me write my book in the garden all day, and sit in the short bath in the evening drinking hot cider she boiled in a saucepan to strengthen it, and singing duets with the boy in his bed across the passage.

I had been reading Nathanael West's *The Day of the Locust*. I wanted to write about how people whom you have the strength to help can destroy you if you are not quite strong enough. The novel, *Thursday Afternoons*, also accommodated one of the missionary nurses, who was cowishly aroused, without knowing what to do about it, by any and all of the male doctors, an unpersonable bunch of left-overs which was all that were available to our non-priority hospital in the desperate wartime shortage.

I was in Casualty once when one of the vaguer ones started to open up the wrong leg of a boy with an abscess. He carefully sprayed the right place with local anaesthetic, waited for it to take effect, and when I had turned away to get something, made a stab for the wrong leg with his scalpel.

The boy's yell brought Sister in. She pushed the doctor out, and opened the abscess swiftly and neatly herself.

When I was on night duty in the children's ward at Christmas, this same doctor brought me a child's mug of what he called Christmas cocktail. It looked like orange juice, but it was laced with raw alcohol and ether. When he had gone, I took a large swallow and instantly fell flat on my back in the middle of the ward. I came to some time later with children crawling over me like Gulliver in Lilliput, and the small ones in cots standing rattling the bars and mewing, 'Nurth Dickie, Nurth Dickie.'

Coming back early one morning from a night off at 52, I found the hospital porter out in the street, staring up at the sky.

'Get inside, nurse! Get inside!'

'What is it – bombers?'

'They're coming over without pilots! They're coming over without pilots!' He jumped about and waved his arms. He was very agitated.

So were we all when we found out what the V.1 Doodlebugs were. No one who lived through that time will ever forget the ponderous 'De dum, de dum,' as the evil thing, obscenely cruci-form, lumbered overhead, while you dived for cover, fell on your face, or just stood and hunched your shoulders. When the engine cut out, it fell. Silence. A whistling. The explosion. The enormous relief: They didn't get me, followed by guilt at being relieved that they got somebody else.

Sister Doucette issued orders that when a Doodlebug was heard approaching, all mobile patients should dive under their beds. Each nurse should throw herself on top of the nearest immobile patient, with a pillow over her head.

'De dum, de dum, de dum, de dum.' Miss Fletcher ran for the lavatory. Patients began to scramble under their iron beds. I dived under the bed of the fattest woman in the ward, and met Sister Doucette coming in from the other side.

When the Doodlebugs were still coming inexorably, and the first V.2 rocket fell on a Woolworths on a Saturday morning south of the river, the Homoeo evacuated some of its patients and staff to one of the large pseudo-country houses on Coombe Hill, near Kingston. A mullioned and turreted sham baronial castle was converted into a hospital by putting beds into the large ground floor rooms, an operating table in the master's study, private patients in the bedrooms, and nurses in the servants' quarters.

There were two day sisters and staff nurses, but no Matron or Ass. Mat. At night, one nurse and a probationer looked after the whole place. I was the nurse, since I was past my second year and on my way to Finals.

One of us would roam round the shadowy rooms, where dark portraits of purchased ancestors kept watch over the beds, which were kept away from the panelling by blocks in the unlikely event that the war might end and the people return to occupy the house again. The other sat in the cavernous flag-stoned hall, with a one-bar electric fire stirring the breezes that came under the heavy oak door. I liked the feeling of responsibility and independence. We were all more relaxed. The patients used to sweep the wards for us and help in the kitchen, cooking their own breakfast when their families brought eggs.

We had a resident woman doctor, and the surgeons came down once or twice a week to operate in what cannot have been a very sterile theatre. All the furniture and books and pictures had been removed from the study, and we hung clean sheets over the walls on operating day.

On Mr Tucker's gastric day, when he went into a corner and put his rubbered hands together to pray, he looked like Madonna of the Snows, with his white gown and cap and his pale, intense face against the sheets.

He was an innovator of what is now common practice, making patients move as soon as possible after a major operation. To a patient who had struggled free of the anaesthetic to find that while he was unconscious somebody had sewn his navel to his backbone, the nurse who brought the news that Mr Tucker had ordered him out of bed was a sadist.

One evening, Sister, giving me her report, told me, 'Mr Tucker says that when that partial gastrectomy in the library wakes, he's to be stood out of bed.'

He was a pleasant clerkly man with whom I had chatted early that morning as I shaved and prepped him before I went off duty. He had told me about his wife, whose nerves were not strong, about the daughter who took piano lessons, and the other daughter who played football and was more like a boy.

'Are you nervous?'

'No, I –' he examined his feelings. 'No, I don't think so, nurse. I'll be so glad to get rid of the pain. My wife always said it was because I eat too fast. It gets on her nerves.'

When I went round the six beds in the bay-windowed library, his eyes were open, watching me.

'How do you feel?'

'All right.' He munched his dry mouth. 'Can I have a drink?'

'I'm sorry. Not yet.' I wiped his coated lips with a wet cloth and let him suck the corner.

'Nurse.' He turned his eyes up at me. 'I wish I'd not had it done.'

'I've got an injection for you. Are you very uncomfortable?'

'It's just bearable if I don't move.'

I was caught in that kind of dilemma that often troubled me: whether to follow my instinct or the doctor's orders, if I thought they were wrong for a certain situation. It seemed madness to disturb the poor fellow. On the other hand, if a surgeon could not rely on the nurses to carry out instructions, how could he take the responsibility?

At two o'clock, I still had not decided. I wanted to debate it with Nurse George, the plump young probationer, who had been going cheerfully round the house in slippers, tucking people in like a mother, and making cups of tea for those who could not sleep. But when I was as new as she was, I did not like it if a senior nurse mused, 'I wonder if we should . . .', or, 'I'm not sure whether . . .' It made me feel insecure.

The partial gastrectomy, awake off and on and restless, was the only ill patient we had. The other two post-ops were appendicectomies who slept all night, right through hourly pulse taking.

It was a cold, still night. Georgie and I ate our sandwiches in the hall, where we could hear patients anywhere in the house, and she told me about life in Peterborough, and her father's nail factory, and her sister's eighteen hour labour with her second.

After going to look at the gastrectomy, she came back to report that he was sleeping. Perhaps I would leave him alone until morning, and stand him up about seven, just before the day staff came on, which would technically count as having done it during the night. At five when I checked his pulse, he was awake, propped up, staring at the mullioned window, outside which the still cedars waited blackly for the night to be over.

'How do you feel?'

He considered himself inwardly. 'All right.' He was the sort of man who would try to say, 'All right' even if he was dying.

'You can have another injection. Would you like it now?'

'All right.'

'But you know, all Mr Tucker's patients have to stand out of bed within twelve hours after an operation. I hate to do this to you, but I'm afraid it's orders. Why don't we do that now, and then I'll give you your morphia and I won't need to bother you before I go off duty. All right?'

'All right.'

As I helped him to sit up, his eyes widened with pain, and he said, 'Ow,' and apologized. I had put a towel on the floor so we need not bother with slippers, and with the covers back, I helped him to swing his legs very cautiously over the side of the bed. He sat with them dangling, leaning weakly against me, getting used to the stiffness and pain of his assaulted midriff.

'Is that enough?' he gasped. 'Do we have to go the whole way?'

I could have said 'No', but I said, 'I'm afraid so.'

'I want to do what's best.' Sitting on the edge of the mattress, he got his toes on the towel, gripping tightly on to my arm. He tried weight on his feet. Suddenly his grip became a vice. 'Oh, Christ. Oh, Jesus.' All in a moment, his face was green. He stared at me in astonishment.

I heard Georgie in the passage and called her. She helped me to get him back in the bed. He was passing out with the pain. I gave him the morphia, and sent Georgie to telephone the cottage in the grounds where the doctor slept.

Dr Werner, who was an exiled German, came running with a coat over pyjamas. She was fairly young and not very experienced.

'Something has let go,' I told her, and she sent us hurrying to set up a drip. She was anxious and panicky. She nearly killed me when a fleck of foil from the cap went into the neck of the saline bottle and we had to open another.

She went to telephone Mr Tucker, and then stayed with the patient. The drip kept blocking. With that type of equipment, it was not always your fault if it got an air lock, but she cursed me for a fool. Beyond the screens, the other patients lay awake and uneasy, not daring to ask what was wrong. When I came back from temperatures and dressings at seven, the man was awake and yet not awake, his eyes open, not knowing me, his abdomen already spread into the telltale pear shape of peritonitis.

I did not want to go off duty, but when the day nurses came on, the patient was their property, and Day Sister, after asking, 'What on *earth* has been going on?' chased me away.

I went to bed. There was nothing else to do, and slept in and out of nightmare. At noon, one of the nurses came upstairs in her lunch time and sat on my bed.

I woke in fright.

'He's dead,' the nurse said. 'Mr Tucker wouldn't operate. He said it was too late.'

Nobody blamed me, but that makes no difference, when you are blaming yourself.

That evening, Mr Tucker did a post mortem. There was no place to do this in the Coombe Hill house, so he did it in the garage on the carpentry bench, with another nurse and me holding up stable lanterns, as there was no electricity. Dr Werner was there with a torch, and she saw what Mr Tucker saw after he cut down into the abdomen and released a flood of evil-smelling fluid.

When I went into the library that night, not looking at the clean, empty bed, the men were quiet and thoughtful. I was brusque with them, because I thought they saw me as a murderer. I hardly spoke to Georgie as we went about the business of getting our survivors settled for the night. At nine o'clock, dim wartime headlights curved round the drive. I unbolted the front door. Two women stood there, one about forty, one older.

'Excuse me,' the younger one said. 'We would have come sooner, but the car wouldn't start. They told us to come for my husband's things.'

'Come in. I'll get the other nurse.' I could not stay and talk to them.

Next morning, Dr Werner came into the kitchen where we

were having breakfast, fried by Mr Jones, an ambulating hernia.

'Are you the only nurse in this place who can type?' she asked me.

'As far as I know.' I had typed some medical papers for her.

'Then it will have to be you. Bring your typewriter to the cottage as soon as you've finished your meal.'

She wanted me to type the report of the post mortem. I took it down straight on to the typewriter, while she paced the room, dictating. She was very jittery. When we got to the bit about what Mr Tucker had observed when he cut down to the site of surgery, she started a sentence four times.

'No, no. Wait a minute. Let me think.'

I waited. After two more false starts, she said, 'Oh damn, I don't want to do this now. And you're tired. I can finish this later. It doesn't really have to be typed.'

I do not know what was finally written in the report, nor who saw it. I was moved back to London on a medical ward, so I did not have any more of Mr Tucker's patients.

Soon after V.E. Day, I left the hospital before taking my State finals. The rumour was out that State Registered nurses would not be released for at least five years.

There is a picture of me taken that summer in a swim suit, a total skeleton. All the nurses at the hospital were too thin, except those who were too fat. We were all exhausted. Most of us had stopped menstruating, and we all had boils and septic fingers. I had seven at one time, done up in separate bandages.

11

After the war, Doady's husband went back to his practice in London. They could not find a house, and so she brought her family of four back to live for a while at 52.

Minnie Maunder had gone to live with her married daughter. Fanny could not find any servants, so Doady and I ran the unwieldy establishment between us.

52 had always been a centre of warmth and security, not only for us, but for many cousins who wished that Fanny was their mother, and for dozens of family and friends who dropped in frequently, and gathered there on ritual occasions. Chilworthy had long been sold, and 8 Mulberry Walk divided into flats. In 1933, Henry's father had been hit by a motorcycle while he was crossing Chelsea Embankment at his usual place and by his usual method of holding up his walking stick and stepping out into the road. Seven years later, the Mater followed the Guvnor, ending her long vigil of grief for her youngest son by going to join him. Fifty-two had become the focal point for the family. It had always been the focus for Doady and me, even after she got married and I went to King Edward VII Hospital. Coming back to work in it now, looking up at it from the different viewpoint of the basement, it began to be more tyrant than friend.

The war was over. Men of all ages, often to be found nursing a remedial gin or sherry in Fanny's drawing room, were coming back to jobs and women that sometimes were not there.

The low-proof gin wore curious labels. The sherry tasted of furniture polish. Clothes had Austerity tags. The black market prospered. There was a shortage of everything, except government regulations. Everyone was exhausted. They stopped being friendly to strangers, and threw out Churchill, who had saved their lives. Henry hung up his tin hat and A.R.P. arm band on the wall of his dressing room, and planted a rock garden on the roof of the air-raid shelter. Fifty-two was supposed to be back in its normal routine, except that there was now no Ellen Page or Nanny Gathergood or Mary Lott or Dowson or Annie Bavin or Majer to run it.

Minnie Maunder still came every morning, trustworthy as the dawn, and Doady and I made feeble attempts to keep the house civilized. We shared the cooking and cleaning, and carried the arm-stretching red tin trays up and down the worn lino of the back stairs. Since I fell about every sixth trip, Fanny's sets of glass and china began to be eroded piece by piece. The gravy tureen had no handles. One of the vegetable dish lids had to be put on in two sections.

The children slept in the basement, and the kitchen was the centre of their world, as the nursery had been for us. For Henry, the basement had been a place he only visited to go to his wine cellar, or the dark room where he developed and enlarged his hundreds of photographs. But he had been somewhat democratized by the war, which had swept away many of the traditional customs he had been brought up to consider as vital as breathing. When Doady and I struck against carrying lunch for nine people up to the dining room, he agreed to Sunday lunch in the kitchen with food slapped from stove to table.

With his new-found democracy, Henry became increasingly involved in the work of the Royal Borough of Kensington. The Kensington Town Hall acquired the same sort of mystique as the North Kensington Lawn Tennis Club. It was his *place*. The week revolved round committee meetings of the Borough Council, the only power on earth, including Hitler, which could make him change his eight o'clock dinner time.

In the desperate need for housing after the war, he caused some good blocks of Council flats to be built on the far side of the curving Lansdowne streets that once were a race course. The estate is called Henry Dickens Court. The buildings are named after characters from Charles Dickens, but they stand as a memorial to the industry of his grandson, hammering against the fearful odds of bureaucracy. When the Queen Mother came for the official dedication of the estate, Henry was on the platform with her in his fur-lined Alderman's robe, and afterwards they had tea together in 4 Dombey House, with Mrs Langham pouring.

Tea with Royalty became quite an addiction. Some years later, when Queen Elizabeth visited Beaumont College, his school at Old Windsor, the oldest living Old Boy was among the few invited to have tea with her. Henry sat next to the Queen, and she poured.

I was staying at 52 with my husband and children. That evening, after he came back from Beaumont, Henry sat on at the dinner table with the port decanter after Roy had gone to write letters, and I had gone down to the kitchen to watch television with the housekeeper, Mary Vinton, who now lived there. I came up much later with silver and glasses to put away. Thinking Henry might be asleep in his armchair before the dining room fire, I opened the door quietly.

He was sitting at the table in his old black velvet smoking jacket, pipe ash on his waistcoat, his pince-nez halfway down his nose, looking over them at nothing with his faded blue eyes. He did not see or hear me.

'The Queen.' He thumped the table gently with his fist. 'The Queen, the Queen. My God, the Queen. I've absolutely fallen in love with her.'

He still drove a solid box on wheels, a grey Vauxhall that had spent most of the war propped up on blocks in Doady's barn. It had two little arms that flipped out on either side for turning signals. The switch was chancy, and sometimes they did not flip out, or flipped out both together, so that the driver behind had to guess. Henry preferred hand signals anyway. He always drove with his window open, so that he could give the imperious halt sign, or pat down pushy drivers, or give the circular wave to timid ones. When Fanny drove with him in winter, she wore fur boots and gloves and a woollen shawl tied over her hat, and wrapped herself in a steamer rug, with a hot water bottle and a thermos of cocoa.

Doady rolled up the window and ferried the children to and

from their local schools. I used the car if I was going out at night, and in the day time I rode the bicycle that used to take me through the chill metallic dawns to Sunbeam Talbot.

Because there was no space or peace to write at home, I bicycled every morning to a borrowed basement flat in a street near what used to be the Holland Park roller skating rink, and wrote a book about a man I had nursed at the Homoeo, who had an amputated leg, and used to talk to me at night when he could not sleep, about what it was like to be immobilized.

When it was done, the situation at 52 was still fairly clotted, so I started another book, to keep me out of the house all day. The owner of the Holland Park refuge had returned, so a friend of Fanny's who lived in Knightsbridge let me work in an empty room the size of a cupboard. I was thirty. Time to start getting nostalgic, and to write about atmospheres of childhood. I began to write a novel about the Portobello Road.

Since I was born and brought up on that corner of Chepstow Villas, the Porto, which flows beside the house like one of those garbage-carrying streams which come from the hillside along the wall of an Italian villa, was always a part of my life.

There was the newspaper shop from which *The Times* and *Morning Post* and *Daily Mirror* (for the kitchen) were delivered with a rattle and thud through the letter box. Opposite in a triangular corner of the high bakery building, was a normal sized man known as the little shoemaker, hammering away with nails in his mouth on a metal last shaped like a foot.

The size of a tradesperson was not a matter of height. When you bought a dress at Harrods or Harvey Nichols, you had it fitted by a sad pale woman with pungent armpits and a pin-cushion on her black dress where her heart should be. The darts and hems were then sewn by the store's dressmakers. Neither the fitters nor the sewers were little women. A little woman might be six foot two, but she was in business for herself, often in her own home.

She was referred to in the possessive. 'My little dressmaker', or, 'Gerty's little woman who makes slip covers', or 'Nan

116

1. Sir Henry Fielding Dickens, K.C., K.C.B.E., and Lady Dickens –
'The Guvnor and the Mater' – by the mulberry tree at 8 Mulberry
Walk, Chelsea.

2. The Dickens family – Elaine, Olive, my grandmother Maire Dickens,
Gerald, Enid, my grandfather Henry Fielding Dickens, my father
Henry Dickens and (in front) Ceddy, Pip.

3. My grandparents,
Herman and Emma
Runge, Chilworthy,
1911. He is dressed as an
English squire. She is in
her wicker sentry box.

4. My brother Gerald (Bunny) with his cousin Eddie Carbutt, at
Chilworthy, 1910.

5. Henry and Fanny on holiday to take the cure, Aix-les-Baines, 1925.

6. Three sisters – VV and Dusa Roche, Marie Dickens, at 8 Mulberry Walk.

8. Henry in the Tennis Tournament, Coq-sur-Mer.

7. With Doady at Chilworthy, me three and a half, Doady 5.

9. Trying to prevent love between my brother and my best friend. Family holiday, Göteborg, Sweden, 1933.

10. The little shoemaker's shop in the Portobello Road, taken over by the Italian's art gallery.

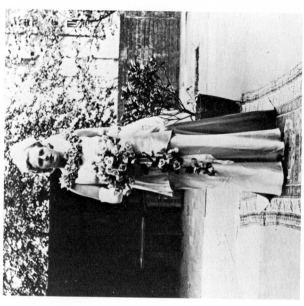

12. Débutante going to Court. In the back yard of 52.

11. At Chilworthy, with Doady, and Bunny as a naval cadet.

14. 52 Chepstow Villas, after a little tree man had butchered the plane trees.

13. Following the Fleet – in boiler suits. Seaview, I.O.W.

15. With Pam on Bobby, North Falmouth, 1954.

16. Researching a story about a circus rider for *Woman's Own*.

17. With Jo at the cottage
in Hinxworth.

18. With the cast of 'Follyfoot', Steve Hodson, Arthur English,
Desmond Llewellyn, Gillian Blake, Christian Rodska (on bike).

19. N-a-a-s Diggins in hospital uniform, 1940.

20. Reading to children at Hinxworth.

21. In the doorway of the cottage.

22. With readers of *Woman's Own*.

23. On the steps of 52. Fanny with Prudence, Mary Vinton with Pam, Minnie Maunder.

24. Henry at Gerty's cottage.

25. Roy – on right – a commissioned officer in the U.S. Navy.

26. Roy – age 21 – a sailor in the U.S. Navy.

27. With Pamela and
    Prudence: a return to
    Chilworthy in 1964.

28. Fanny at her sister Gerty's cottage.

29. *This is Your Life*, with my publisher Charles Pick and Eamonn Andrews.

30. With some of the family at 52. Christopher Dickens (Bunny's son), Roy, Philip Danby, Doady, Fanny, Henry, Mary Danby.

31. The North Falmouth house in winter.

32. With Roy, Henry and Fanny, on the terrace at North Falmouth.

Harris's little smocker'. There were little men too, who did odd jobs of carpentry or French polishing or wireless repairs, or put heels and soles on shoes, like the little man at the top of the Portobello Road.

Beyond him was the Cricketers, aptly named, where the beer was fetched in jugs for the men after the Sunday game in the backyard. Then the sweetshop where you could buy peardrops which smelled of acetone, and a penn'orth of sulphur-coloured sherbet powder to dip a licked finger into. The Lord Nelson was on the next corner. Men came out of an alley at the side, buttoning up their trousers. At night, they roistered up the hill and milled under the lamp post at the corner of Chepstow Villas, bawling songs without consonants. Allowed to sleep in my brother's front cabin room when he was away, I held my breath in the bunk under the window until they had moved on up the road to meet the singing rabble weaving down it from the Sun in Splendour.

From the night nursery at the back, the street was too far away to hear the singing. But in summer when windows were open, you heard over the rooftops women screaming, babies crying, men cursing, and hacking coughs that ended in sounds of vomiting.

From where the Porto began to wind downhill on the other side of Archer Street, it was known locally as the Lane. There was an ironmongers that smelled of paraffin and firewood, and a grocer on the corner who let us dip scoops into the bins of brown sugar and currants. Fanny also dealt with Whiteleys who delivered in horse vans, and Hawes at Notting Hill Gate who had a boy with a bicycle. When she wanted to take her children for a walk, and to pick up something for Ellen Page or Minnie, we went down the Lane to the little corner grocery. Beyond it was a larger shoe shop, where I learned how to steal nails from the open boxes, and one of the new Woolworths, where everything cost 3d or 6d, and I also practised picking up small items.

My desire was not so much for the celluloid dolls and half-inch nails, as for the forbidden thrill of crime. When I was old enough to go to Confession, 'examination of conscience' meant raking over one's behaviour for something that would not be the same old sins month after month, I remembered those infant robberies, and produced them at St Mary of the Angels, hoping to shock. The priest at Smelly Angels, who used to read his letters during children's confessions, told me that it was not a sin at that age. Oh hell. He would not even bother to forgive it.

Farther down was the Salvation Army Temple, a foetid cinema where we were not allowed to look at the stills in cracked glass cases, a butcher selling highly coloured meat and the high brown convent wall on which somebody had chalked 'Nuns prison'.

Ever since memory, the Portobello Road market has happened on Saturday mornings. In those early days when we ran down for a paper of sherbet, or walked in kilts and tams to the corner grocery with Fanny, it was still literally a flea market. All along the gutter, rickety stalls and barrows were piled with rags, torn jerseys, mismated shoes, chipped china, bent tin trays, three-legged furniture and unfunctioning appliances from the early days of electricity.

The market did not start until two streets down from Chepstow Villas, respectable with its nannies and hearthstoned steps and plane trees pollarded down to the nub by somebody's little man who did trees. At the far end of the street where the nuns were incarcerated, it became vegetable and fruit stalls, buzzing with bluebottles, and it was here that Doady and I got involved with one of the small gangs of boys who roamed those lower reaches of the Lane. It was a very innocent gang. A few sweets pinched, every chocolate and cigarette machine pummelled and kicked, a penny cadged from a man reeling out of a pub, Button B pressed in all the telephone boxes because Harry Housego had once released a flood of coppers.

We were allowed to play in the street and have the boys home to play in the yard. From the corner of the mews wall, we found a way to travel all the way to the Lord Nelson, over the roofs and along the tops of walls without touching the ground.

As the years changed, so did the Portobello Road. The stalls began to sell more useful things. Victorian flowered jugs and basins and yellow wooden washstands, sour with the damp of hasty washings in cold bedrooms. Tables and chairs and wrecked harmoniums. Meat covers, tapestry stools, brass jugs, old 78 records, a suit of armour. People began to come from farther away to wander along the stalls and look for bargains. They discovered that the vegetables and fruit on the costers' barrows at the end of the Lane were better and cheaper than in the shops.

As late as 1960 you could still find bargains, and still haggle over prices with stallholders who thought you were a mug if you paid them what they asked. After the Porto was discovered by tourists, and every antique shop in Church Street or Chelsea put up a satellite stall, there were no more Saturday morning bargains. You can still find fascinating things there, like musical boxes with bristly metal reels and lustre jugs and old sporting prints, but you pay no less than they are worth, and often more. You can still haggle – this gives the visitor from Houston, Tokyo or West Berlin the genuine thrill – but the stallholders with grubby nails who sport the specially tarnished, rather faggy Portobello Road accent only allow you to beat them down to the price they were going to charge you anyway.

When the whole world began to flock to the Lane on Saturdays, the stalls crept higher and higher, until they washed right across Chepstow Villas, on up past the church hall where we were Brownies, as far as our old garage by the Sun in Splendour, bought by a Free French mechanic during the war and known as 'Garage du Maquis'. The market went indoors as well as outdoors. The newspaper shop became a place where they sold brass ship fittings and roundabout horses and curly notices that said, 'Oh Look!' and, 'Longest Ride at the Fair!' The sweetshop sold marble busts and rather elegant reproduction furniture. The Cricketers overflowed with people in turtlenecks drinking barley wine and lager and lime and talking Dutch and French and Saudi Arabian. The yard of the Lord Nelson was a youth arcade of T shirts and torn lace dresses and old Army overcoats and mess jackets.

The little shoemaker's tiny triangular workshop was leased by a little Italian who sold amateurish paintings of children with big heads, maidens in woods and praying hands. On a fine Saturday morning, he would prop his gallery against the ironwork on top of the wall that curved round the corner to the front gate of 52.

'My God, man!' Henry stood at the top of the front steps in his Saturday morning shirtsleeves and braces. 'Take that damned stuff off my wall.'

'Ah, Meester Deekens.' The Italian hung on the gate in a black beret and grinned cheerily at him. 'You like art. You liking me. Habudda leetla glassa gin?'

'Take that filthy stuff off my wall, or I'll call the police.'

But round about twelve-thirty, when Henry poured an aperitif before the Saturday sausage lunch for any family or friends who happened to be in the market, the Italian would be there having a gin, not quite inside the house, but on one of the stone seats of the porch.

One winter when my husband and I were in London and our small daughters were going to the convent school in Chepstow Villas, they used to stand on the corner of the Porto on Saturday mornings and peddle the holy pictures the nuns gave them.

Just as the Portobello Road has had a fluctuating pattern and style, Chepstow Villas has gone up and down over the years. Most of the solid square plastered houses were built at the beginning of the nineteenth century. Fifty-two was lived in by Napoleon's cousin. There is a plaque on a house opposite: 'Louis Kossuth 1802–1894, Hungarian patriot, stayed here'. When I was a child, it was quite a decent address, if one *had* to live on that side of the Park. In the late Thirties, it began to go downhill. Family houses were broken into flats and bed-sitting rooms. Front gardens were concreted over, or filled up with rubbish. Snobbish at seventeen, I did not want to invite new people home, because it was such a dingy neighbourhood.

After a raffish post-war period when there were clubs and drugs and squatters, it began to be rediscovered, and now it is right up there again as a very acceptable address, the houses painted and the gardens planted, the dingy top stretch of the Portobello Road, originally workmen's cottages, transformed into expensive chic little town houses for lucky young couples and people who work in embassies.

Fifty-two itself, when we had to sell it after Henry and Fanny died, was bought by discriminating people who have turned it into the elegant house it should have been with us – or should it? They have made the improvements we always talked about. By making Henry's ground floor dressing room the kitchen, they have saved that crippling climb with trays up the back stairs. They painted and carpeted the top lavatory and threw away the filthy bit of crumpled newspaper that kept the draught out of the ventilator grill. Central heating has eliminated the broken gas fires in the bedrooms and the mantelpiece whose side was scarred by Henry's pumps as he sat on the bottom of his spine in the old armchair he had at Cambridge, warming the undersides of his legs at the dining room fire.

Going back to visit 52, I found the backyard grassed over, and the air raid shelter, tomb of stray cats after the war, demolished. No one knows what happened to the rock garden plants brought back from Italy in Fanny's spongebag.

My brother's cabin is a dressing room. The new children play and sleep in the basement, and cannot lie under the window and watch the plane tree branches stir across the square panes of the street lamps. Well, those old green street lamps, converted from the gas lights at which the lamplighter used to tilt his pole, have not been there for years. The busy road, an unofficial by-pass of Notting Hill Gate, is lit by tall staring cranes of metal and concrete. The one opposite 52 is still blacked out on one side, because it kept Alderman Dickens awake.

As you go in at the front door now, the great sunk doormat is still there. The stained glass inner door is gone. The high brown doors are painted white and have graceful handles instead of embossed brass knobs. Minnie's polished lino is gone, and the chandelier which she and Mary Lott dissected each August when Henry took the cure at Abano or Aix-les-Bains. But the atmosphere is indestructible. I stood in the hall and felt the lingering love and safety, and the echo of a voice down the stairs.

'Is that you, Monty?'

The nice woman who lives there now told me that she agonized over the double marble basins. She had wanted to design her elegant new bathroom around them, but the decorator decreed that they must go, along with the *One Pair of Hands* geyser and the rusted tank and chain in the top lav.

In the small bare room in Knightsbridge, I wrote *Joy and Josephine* about the Portobello Road and the way it used to be, and that whole neighbourhood.

I thought I had got it out of my system, but it keeps turning up again in books, as nurses and hospitals do. Twelve years later, after I had written a book that people did not much like, and was struck low, empty of ideas, and thought I was on the skids, Roland Gant, friend and editor, spent a wet Wednesday afternoon going round my old haunts with a camera. He sent to me in America alluring photographs of 52, with Henry's Vauxhall in front of it, advertisements for 'models' outside the newspaper shop at the top of Pembridge Road, an old lady in black coming out of Smelly Angels, the Garage du Maquis and demolition sites for Council flats and the new Notting Hill Gate Underground station.

I went to England to write *The Heart of London* about this changing neighbourhood. Where the harmless drunks used to bawl their way home, arms linked, there were now riots and nightly street fights between West Indians with knives and Teddy Boys swinging bicycle chains. Many of the terrace streets were exploited by sharp slum landlords into crammed lodgings for shivering immigrants who wished they had not come, but could not afford to go back. Drug pushers moved in. The slow fusty stores changed into coffee bars and cheap clothes shops that changed again in a few months.

But the tree blossom in Ladbroke Square still fell on the citified grass where young mothers unpacked picnics. Fifty-two lurching a little under a leaking roof, stood like a rock while the waters of change flowed turgidly by. The second hand shop with the sign 'Second Hand Clothes. Misfits. Uniforms. Waiters. Weddings. Riding Clothes Bought and Sold', where at eleven I had coveted a pair of enormous riding boots, had been moved round the corner, but intact, with the same sign, and what looked like the same pair of boots.

12

Doady and I muddled on, depressed at 52. It was no longer funny when the boiler in the kitchen went wrong and we had to send for the plumber who kept screws and nuts in his beret. A faithful man got tired of calling for me at the back door with his bowler hat and umbrella, and went off to marry somebody else. A lot of things were still rationed, and those that were not were unobtainable. The Ministry of Food could not find jobs for all the people in the rationing offices, so it looked as if we were stuck for ever with bacon and sugar coupons, and beating soya flour into the butter to make it taste worse, but go farther. We speculated that the conquered Germans were probably already living better than we were.

I was writing a weekly column for a women's magazine. The Ministry of Information invited a group of women journalists to visit the cities of Bremen and Hamburg, so that we could write articles about how German women were living.

We went by boat to Bremerhaven and by train to Hamburg. Everything was flat. Totally flat. As far as you could see, there was nothing except the tall concrete bunkers that had been built as air raid shelters.

Our guide, a woman of about twenty-five who looked forty, took us into one of the bunkers, a honeycomb of thick-walled cells, with six or seven people living in each. Outside one of them, a woman spoke to me and pulled me inside. The cell, like all of them, smelled like the sewer of a charnel house. On the single bunk, her husband lay asleep or in a coma, his sharp white nose pointing at the low concrete ceiling.

'My man is very ill,' the woman told me in good English. 'You must help.'

I touched him. 'I'm afraid he's dead.'

'No.' She was quite old and ugly, with a fat mole on one side of her nose, the only well nourished thing about her.

I stumbled out under the low opening. In the next cell, a woman sat cross legged in the doorway, the only floor space. Behind her, children played on the concrete, and a young boy lay on the bunk with eyes shut, smoking.

'Diese Frau ...' All my German, so carefully learned for exams at St Paul's, left me. 'Ihre Mann . . . tod . . .'

Her eyes were almost as dead as the man's next door.

'Man mussen –' I used some word for taking away, the wrong word. She shrugged.

In Bremen, part of the town was standing. Shops were even open in what would have been a fairly normal way, if there had been anything in them beyond empty cotton reels, single shoes, bleached advertisements for bread. We stayed in an Army hut. I shared a room with a woman from one of the home magazines, who cried in the night. The food was mostly pieces of bread spread, because we were special visitors, with rancid lard.

Fanny's family came from this area. With the help of the guide, I tracked down one of my relations, and we sent a small boy messenger. She came to supper. There was some kind of processed meat like compressed sawdust, re-boiled cabbage and a basket of stale rolls. We put all the rolls into Fanny's cousin's big bag, and the women added brooches, a watch, a gold pencil, cigarettes. I caught myself feeling pleased that we had helped her. But it was Fanny's *cousin* that I was patronizing.

After we got home, I did not write anything about how women lived in Bremen and Hamburg. I don't think any of us did.

At 52 Doady and I quarrelled, as we had not since we were rival children, over stupid things like burned saucepans. Her growing boys were loud and restless. Mary insulted the good woman who took her for walks. Henry and Fanny were increasingly bothered by the noise and commotion and overcrowding. Like pigs in a crammed pen, we would all have killed each other if it had gone on much longer.

Houses and flats were scarce and expensive, but at last Doady's husband found a house in Wimbledon and she and the children moved out. Fifty-two was left battered, and eerily silent. Mrs Catchpole agreed to come and work for Henry and Fanny, because she could not find anywhere else to live with her young daughter.

Walking through Hanover Square on the way to the cinema, I turned on an impulse into an estate agent's office and saw a picture of a cottage in Hertfordshire. It was three hundred years old, three farm cottages made into one, with a heavy thatch like eyebrows and an air of having grown up out of the ground, instead of being built on top of it.

One of the things you could not get after the war was a car. Through an advertisement in a Kensington paper, I had bought for a thieving sum a red open car with a broken back window and a torn hood that took half an hour to get down on a fine day, or up when it was raining. If it was down, it stayed down, but when it was up the bolts might fly open if you went over a bump, and the roof would recoil, not all the way down, but standing straight up in the air like the hood of a cobra.

It ran for a while and then collapsed in the middle of the street like a worn out cart horse. At the post mortem, the crankcase was found to be a network of tiny cracks, pinned together with makeshift rivets that would have broken the heart of Sid Whiffen.

Just before the red car died, I drove it out to Hertfordshire one gentle summer evening, with the sun lowering behind Barnet.

I drove through Baldock past the big nylon factory – nylons! another item that was still as rare as radium – and left the Cambridge road at the corner where the overhanging cottages have been threatening to fall into the street for centuries. Up a hill and down a hill and there, just as the woman had said on the telephone, was the small sign saying diffidently, 'Hinxworth'. The red car was sputtering a bit as I drove along a narrow lane, with an increasing sense of familiarity. It was not just that I had seen the charming photograph of the cottage. But I knew, as I turned right by the vicarage wall, down a slight slope between heavy elms, saw the neat grass outside the clipped hedge and stopped by the gate, I knew what waited for me at the end of the cobbled path.

The house was the colour of pale apricots. Without noticing particular plants, there was the impression of flowers everywhere, hollyhocks, roses, phlox. Outside the open door between two big rosemary bushes, a woman was sitting in a low chair. The sun had gone down, but the apricot house was lit with a kind of afterglow that coloured the small window panes and edged the grey of the woman's hair. She smiled peacefully. How could she smile if she was going to leave this place and let me live here?

I was going to live here, of course. I had known that since I saw the photograph in the office in Hanover Square.

I moved into the cottage a few months later. I had no furniture, and no money left after buying the house. I brought my bed from the old day nursery, and found some odd bits of stuff at Mr Gottlieb's trading post in Archer Street.

It was a big double-fronted shop, jammed from the back wall to the windows with armour, oak chests, iron grates, cracked portraits, broken gramophones and musty stuffed furniture. Some of the chairs were out on the pavement, with Mr Gottlieb and his son sitting on them backwards. It would have taken a week to get at things that were at the bottom and back of the heap inside, but with their help, I dragged out some rugs, an armchair and three chests, since the cottage had ceilings that sloped too low for cupboards, and Mr Gottlieb forced on me a quantity of wrought iron lamps, which I was too excited to resist.

The four years I spent at the cottage in Hinxworth seem like much more. I wrote two books while I was there, had ten horses and ponies at various times and experienced all the emotions and events of discovering how to live alone. I was usually by myself during the week. People came at weekends, and a lot of children.

Henry and Fanny came often. As with everything they did, there was an unchanging ritual to their visits.

Fanny came on Friday mornings. I met her train at Hitchin, and we lunched off trays, in the garden or in front of the fire, eating things like pease pudding and semolina with jam, which nobody else liked.

Henry came next morning in his new blue Vauxhall, whose bumpers already curled like moustaches from being caught on the doorposts of his garage in the mews. He left before breakfast to escape traffic, packing the car the night before. To him, a forty mile drive was still in the nature of an expedition, to be prepared for like those remembered European trips in stage coaches, or Grandpa Runge's Lancia Tourer, which had to ascend mountains in reverse, with the passengers trudging.

When I drove him to or from the cottage myself, there were certain way stations at which we stopped for dinks or cups of tea, according to the time of day. Coming from London, we never got farther than the Comet at Hatfield without turning in for a gin and the solitary ice cube in the bucket on the bar. We might stop again at the George and Dragon in Baldock, or take side trips to inspect out-of-the-way churches, or a house he remembered seeing when his parents visited the Lyttons at Knebworth.

Expéditions, pronounced in French, had always been a feature of family life. In Pontresina, where we spent several summers, there was an expédition every day. When we were not struggling up the Piz Palu or the Rosegg or the Diavolezza with ice axes and Henry's weighty camera and glass plates, there would be a brief three hour stroll up the sheer green mountain behind the hotel, or a train ride to the special wild flower valley, or to St Moritz to do the cake shops. From Lenno on Lake Como, a favourite autumn place, there were expéditions galore in the little lake steamers, and a regular short evening excursion up a stony dry wash behind the Hotel San Giorgio.

Drinks, except for wine, were expensive, so Henry kept his own bottles in the bedroom wardrobe. They were perfectly visible to the chambermaid, but the convention was that every few days, Henry made a twilight expedition up the dry wash to dispose of the bottles in a brown paper bag. Signor Capaletti probably watched him go quite tenderly from his office at the back of the hotel.

On fine Saturdays, when he had recovered from the trip to Hinxworth, Henry and I would drive to the top of the Royston downs to poke about among the beech trees and small wild plants that flourish in that chalky turf, and sit comfortably without speaking, with Herts and Beds and Oxford and Gloucestershire rolling away below us to the Bristol Channel. Another Hinxworth tradition was the Sunday visit to the Bushel and Strike in Ashwell, before the big lunch for whoever was down for the weekend or the day. Henry adopted it as Our Pub, in the same way that the Dickens family had taken over the Hôtel de Bruges at Coq-sur-Mer, the Penhelig Arms at Aberdovey, the Poldhu in Cornwall, the banana boat to Jamaica.

Although the cottage was sometimes filled with people at weekends and during Doady's children's holidays, most of the time I was alone with my dog and the cats.

It was the first time in my life that I had ever lived quite alone. I had always lived either at 52 or in a hospital. I had hardly ever spent even one night in a house by myself.

It had taken me a long time to discover my need for solitude. Perhaps I did not need it before. Perhaps I was only ready for it now, after thirty years of bodies and voices and the awareness of breathing presences in the spaces around you while you sleep.

Being alone meant having one plate and one mug, rinsed and upside down on the draining board between meals that were not proper meals, but whatever was left over from the weekend, fried up with an egg.

Reading became more internal. Living with people, you share

a book you like, or talk about it. Alone, it seems written only for you, a secret message. When I met a man who had read all the poetry that sustained me, I was astonished at the coincidence, although most of the poems were known to millions.

Occasionally I felt lonely and unsettled and insecure, and needed people to prove that I existed. I would go to local friends, or up to London.

'What have you been doing with yourself?'

Writing a book. I always was, so that was not news. 'Nothing much. Riding. Gardening.' Watching the poplars.

'Do you ever think about getting married?'

There it was. The assumption that I lived alone perforce, not from choice. I could not wait to get home, where the dog whined behind the door and cats converged from garden waiting places, back to myself, to touch my things, and let the cottage be my assurance of my right to exist.

You went along a cobbled path, either from the road gate or the garage at the side, and brushed between the aromatic rosemary bushes to the front door that was thick, like a church door. It led into the main room of the cottage. The floor was old red tiles, laid straight on to the earth. People said it must be damp, but it was not. The whitewashed walls were so stout that deep cupboards were built into their thickness. In the middle of the room, an oak post that remained from the wall between two cottages was scarred and axe-notched, like the beams overhead, and pocked by some kind of busy borers. As the beams looked as if they had been like that for hundreds of years, it did not seem to matter.

The windows were low, with small lattice panes and windowsills on which you could put geraniums, like a Beatrix Potter illustration. The finest thing about this fine room was the fireplace. It was so wide and deep that you could sit on little benches on either side and look up the chimney. The wide bed of ashes was never cleared. You shovelled away a bucket or two for the rose bed when it got too high. In the winter, the fire never went out. Big logs consorted gently with themselves all night and were bellowed into flame the next morning.

At the back of this fireplace there was a smaller one in the dining room. Beyond was the kitchen, with lavender bushes and a cooking-apple tree outside. The bathroom was on the ground floor. You could lie in the bath with the window open and talk to people on the lawn, and smell the stocks and tobacco plant, with hollyhocks observing you by the wall.

Upstairs were three bedrooms, and an attic over the end of the living room, where the children had beds and no floor space. My room had two windows. The dormer at the back, into which the head of the bed fitted, looked out on an endless stretch of Hertfordshire arable, bounded by dikes, and the small lattice over the front door looked on to my garden and the barley field across the road, and the poplars that stood by the trickle of stream, endlessly turning their leaves this way and that, like hands doing *comme çi, comme ça.*

In the morning, you took your milk can and walked up the hill between the elm trees, past the field where my horses grazed, past the walled rectory garden and the policeman's house and the war memorial and Harry Stanford's thatched cottage, to the dairy shed behind the Clements' house. If May Clements was not there, you stepped down into the cool slate-shelved dairy, lifted the muslin and lowered the dipper into the pan of shuddering fresh milk.

Next was the village pub, the Three Horseshoes, Mr D. Brownfield, lic. to sell beers, wines, spirits, tobacco, where more meetings were held than at the village hall. Beyond that the road to Edworth and the brick council houses where Mrs Morgan lived. She delivered newspapers, and if you had a broom handy, would sweep you through while she was at it. 'I'll just sweep you through' from the front of the house to the back, with a cloud of dust flying out of the kitchen door.

On the right, in the only other street in the village, the post office and shop was big enough for two customers at the same time. A fire guard on the counter protected Hilda Francis from bandits.

When I bought the bungalow next to the cottage, because it had goat sheds which could be turned into stables, Hilda and Fred moved in there and Fred helped me with the horses. Years ago he had driven a funeral hearse with plumed black horses for an undertaker who was prosecuted by the R.S.P.C.A. When it rained, the wet plumes were heavy, but the horses could not drop their heads because of the bearing rein.

The last time I saw plumed horses was at the funeral of Annie Bavin, who had been Granny's lady's maid at Chilworthy and Berkeley Square, and had sewed for us at 52, enjoying such a mighty tea that we used to wonder what she ate for the rest of the week. At the funeral, there was only Fanny and Gerty and me, and Annie's second cousin who had been flushed out from somewhere by her name appearing in the will. Annie's short coffin was borne to and from the church in a carriage with two plumed black horses.

'Annie would have horses,' the second cousin said. 'She allowed for it in her will.'

Beyond the post office shop were two or three larger houses and then the open countryside again, woods and wide fields and hedges that traced the contours of the land into the distance.

This unfashionable, unnoticed corner where Herts and Beds and Cambridgeshire came together was an oasis within reach of London. But there were no weekend people. Everyone lived here and made their living round about.

They could not see how I made my living, since I did not do any visible work.

With all day alone and free to write, I often did not start to work until eight o'clock in the evening. I wrote most of the night, and about four or five, I got into the bath with a mug of tea and a meat paste sandwich and fell asleep. When my chin and bottom lip went under the cooling water, or when the birds outside the bathroom window began their racket, I crawled up the steep stairs on hands and knees and went to bed until Joe barked at the postman, coming up the path at nine o'clock.

If you starve yourself of sleep, it gets back at you at inconvenient moments, like when you are making social conversation, or driving a car. I fell asleep at local dinner parties. I never drove to or from London without pulling off the road at certain spots to have a nap.

Under these idyllic circumstances, I wrote a novel called *Flowers on the Grass*, which began and ended in this cottage.

Ever since I started to write, perhaps before that, I have been intrigued by the idea of alternative lives. At any moment of any of our days, there are choices. We may go this way, or the other. We may keep straight on course or swerve, just slightly perhaps, but the angle widens to a new direction, new people, new developments of ourselves.

What about the choices we don't make? What happens to those alternative selves? Is it possible that they have some sort of shadow existence alongside the one we know, and are in some way realized? Perhaps they have already been realized, although they seem to lie as a choice ahead, since linear time is only an arbitrary physical creation. That would make it easier to understand why certain people and places, glimpsed at the periphery of your own life, are recognizable.

Sometimes when you sense that a strange house has a good feel about it, a happy atmosphere, it may not be because of the people who live in it. They may be at odds. But you could have been happy there. It is one of your alternative places.

Seen from a car or train, certain places draw you. Certain people, glimpsed for a few seconds, can be imagined as yourself. Often the same kind of people and places. With me, it may be a country town street, below a railway bridge, with people shopping. An isolated red brick house that stands in a field and has a woman opening the back door to shake a mop, call a child, throw bread to chickens. Narrow terrace houses in provincial towns or the outer edges of London are very familiar to me, although I have never lived in one.

The story of such a terrace house that has hung about, wanting to be written, but never even started, is of a man riding on a bus, a successful man, perhaps a well-known one – actor, politician, tycoon. Passing this row of houses, he sees a man with an evening paper under his arm, putting his key in the lock. The man on the bus desperately wants to be that person, is sick with longing, not only for the anonymity of that life, but for something he recognizes as familiar to himself.

He gets off the bus at the next stop and walks back to that unremarkable street. At one of the houses that has a stack of bells and names, he asks for a room and starts his alternative life in which he can be anybody he likes, because no one knows him. What happens in the rest of the story, I have no idea. I have never got beyond the place where he gets off the bus.

In the novel I wrote at Hinxworth, I used the idea of a man disappearing from view and leading different lives as a stranger in different settings. The event that pushed him into his wanderings was not the recognition of an unknown place, but suddenly being abandoned by tragedy.

I used a near tragedy from the beginning of the war, when Doady was evacuated to a tiny cottage, with her bed in the sitting room and Ugly lying on it because there was no room anywhere else for his large muscular body. She nearly killed herself and her unborn son by filling an electric kettle when it was not only plugged in, but defective. The baby she was carrying was the one who was blue on the piano at Cookham Dean at Christmas. Perhaps that was why he was blue. He grew into a very intelligent, ambitious and energetic man. Perhaps the electricity did that too.

I also continued to pour out oceans of facile wisdom for *Woman's Own*, for whom I wrote a weekly feature. Serious literary people whom I occasionally met would wonder whether being so closely identified with a magazine that nine million women read in the Tube and the hairdresser's was as bad for the reputation as they hoped it was, since it was obviously good for the bank balance.

Writing for *Woman's Own* gave me a new public, and a journalist's entrée to people and places that interested me. It brought me letters from people all over the world, some of whom I have met, and remain friends with. I continued to write for the magazine long after I had gone to live in America. I used to try to make it sound as if I was still in England most of the time, because it was important to the feature that I was everyone's Monica, who might be met round the corner in the greengrocer's at any moment.

I wrote for *Woman's Own* for twenty years, and then was

thrown out because a thirteen-year-old girl in Liverpool wrote to the editor to complain, quite rightly, that it was time they got some new blood on the magazine.

After living in Hinxworth for a while, I became fascinated with another brand of journalism, the local newspaper. I found myself reading it as I had never read a London paper, from front to back, including all the advertisements and In Memoriams, and the reports of jam contests and meetings of the Arlesey and Stotford Water Board.

The desire was on me to have another job. I went to see the editor of the *Herts Express*, and asked him if he would take me on. I don't know why he did. They had never had a woman reporter before, and as far as the rest of the staff were concerned, they never intended to. But the editor, a cultured, whimsical man, had a whim that day to take a chance, and so I joined the four men in that cluttered, dusty reporters' room, and entered the world of jam contests and water board meetings.

At first I only corrected proofs, endlessly and tediously, and recorrected them when they had been reset, interminably. When you finally pulled the blinds and unplugged the kettle and lifted your coat from the layers of abandoned scarves and old jerseys on the hook behind the door, there was always Bill or Leslie coming through from the comp room with one more roll of galleys.

I also filled inkwells – there was only one typewriter in the office – fetched copy paper from the basement, went out for buns, made the tea and washed up the cracked cups under the cold tap in the lavatory. After a while, I was allowed to reword the ill-written announcements and births, deaths and marriage notices and rewrite the confused reports of darts tournaments and club meetings sent in by local correspondents from the small towns and villages round Hitchen.

The In Memoriams were the only things we were not allowed to alter. You might be itching to get your hands on:

> 'Mother dear
> So far yet so near.
> Her kind face and pleasant ways

People would praise.

Her family at St Ippolyts will be sad on 7th May',

but to rewrite it would be like robbing a grave.

Then I began to be sent out on little jobs, like fêtes and cookery demonstrations. I worked my way through visiting bishops, a new traffic light, the speeches of Council candidates, until after several months I was allowed to go with Arthur to learn Court reporting at Sessions and Assizes in Hertford.

The courtroom was crowded and airless, and the divorces and bigamies and bicycle stealings lost their excitement because of the slow pace of the proceedings. Witnesses were inarticulate or long-winded. Magistrates asked unnecessary questions, to show they were listening, or introduced red herrings, or went to lunch. Counsel at Assizes strung out their time in the limelight. 'Do you seriously mean to tell His Lordship ...' and, 'I must ask you to go in detail once again over the events of that afternoon.'

The reporters on the press benches slept a lot of the time, in relays, so that we could take notes from each other. The first time I was allowed to go alone to Petty Sessions, I spent the next morning making human interest stories out of my notes ('Just give the facts, girl,' from Arthur, reading over my shoulder), and the editor spent the afternoon subbing them into the standard format which made every *Herts Express* story come out the same.

It was my job to ring round all the hospitals once a week to see who had died, and if we had no information in the morgue, to interview the grieving survivors.

'I can't do that. They'll throw me out.' I remembered the Guvnor's funeral, when Henry's brother Pip had knocked a reporter backwards over a gravestone and broken his camera.

'No they won't,' Arthur said. 'They'll give you a cup of tea and a biscuit.'

They did. The power of the *Herts Express* opened doors. The bereaved were glad to see me and my notebook. Most people, apart from my Uncle Pip, do not mind being interviewed, because it gives them a chance to do all the talking.

I went to football matches and bowling and hunt meets and

villages fêtes and horse shows and concerts and weddings and amateur theatricals. I rewrote stuff we stole from other local papers, which meant inventing a new headline and first sentence and changing the order of the facts. I made up competitions for the Children's Corner, and wrote reviews of Westerns and B pictures showing in the local cinema without going to see them.

On press day, I was the one who stayed on late to check the page proofs one more time before they started printing. If I found a mistake after the formes of type were already in place on the huge deafening machine in the basement, Leslie took a hammer and knocked that bit of type so that it would print blurred.

I felt proud of being the one who put the paper to bed, although I was only allowed to do it because Arthur and the others did not want to stay late. When I drove home at last with a fresh damp copy of the *Herts Express* that no alien eyes had yet seen, I felt as if I had produced the whole paper by myself. The other reporters never read it in print, but I still read it from front page to back, even though I had written a lot of it myself, and corrected the proofs for the rest.

When I left the job to write *My Turn to Make the Tea*, I disguised the paper, since I meant to go on living in that corner of Hertfordshire, and I mixed some fiction in with the facts, since I felt that two autobiographical books was all people could stand. It still may be.

When the book came out, I sent a copy to the editor and to Arthur, the reporter with whom I had been most friendly. The editor responded in his polite, cultured way. Arthur did not respond at all, nor give any indication that he had received the book.

Foolishly, with the world-blind egotism of someone who has just had a book published, I rang him up.

'What did you think of the book?'

'What book?'

'The one I sent you.'

'Oh that.' The office sounded busy. I could hear the typewriter stuttering, someone arguing on another telephone, the radio giving out the kind of world news that never got into the *Herts Express*.

'Well?' I had to say it again. 'What did you think?'

'I read some of it,' Arthur said. 'I thought it was silly.'

13

Early in 1951, I hit a low spot in my life. I made some mistakes, and one by one my animals died, as if they had decided they did not want to live with me.

One of the cats fell out of a tree – cats don't fall out of trees – and broke her back. Joe got canine hepatitis and died of heart failure. An indelible memory is of him drooping on the way home from a ride, leaning against the outside of a shop where I had stopped in Ashwell, with the already yellowing white of his eyes turned up at me on the horse. I let him follow me home, instead of sending for Fred in the car.

My thoroughbred horse Bow Window, who had been sold off the track because of his habit of bolting off at right angles during a race and crashing through rails and crowd, broke a leg out hunting. We scrambled up a bank out of heavy ploughland, and the muscular contraction shattered the femur. He staggered at the top of the bank, and I got off and saw his back leg propped awkwardly sideways.

I was at the back of the field, where I always was, partly because I was afraid Bow would run away with me and charge through the hounds, partly because I preferred the jumps after everyone else had crashed them down. Only one or two people saw what had happened, and pulled up. A man who had been following the hunt in a Jeep stopped too and came across the field.

Out of the unbelievable ordeal of getting Bow into a trailer and home, where Fred held him for the vet with the humane killer – I could not touch his muddy bridle for weeks – what emerges is the extraordinary kindness of the Jeep man, who took me back to his wife to be fed and rested and allowed to talk, on and on about the accident.

They went on being friends afterwards. They understood why I had to get another horse immediately, although other people were saying that Monica was such a hypocrite. 'Floods of tears in the hunting field, and two weeks later she's got a new horse.'

I was finished with hunting though. I never should have started. People go out hunting for the excitement of the cross country ride, not because they want to kill foxes, and conveniently close their minds to the cruelty of the chase. Since I was always too far back to see a kill, it was Bow's death rather than the plight of the fox that opened my eyes to its horrors.

I got another dog very soon, and there were other cats, but I still felt heavily depressed, and could not shake off the guilt of responsibility that one always feels for an animal's untimely death.

The discoveries and indulgences of living alone had settled into a pattern that had its cranky, selfish aspects. I was beginning to be bossy with guests. There was my way of doing things, and there was the wrong way. I did not like my routine upset. I did not think that anyone loved me. The children did, of course, but there were nights when I woke sweating with the terror of being everybody's aunt for ever.

And they were growing older. They would not need me. Soon it would be, 'You must go and see Mont.' 'Do we have to?' 'Yes, poor thing, she was so good to you when you were young.' And I would be one of those weathered, horsey women with skin like an old saddle, turning out the same kind of novel every two years and telling incredulous people that I used to be famous.

In alcoholism circles, they say that you have to hit bottom before you can go upwards, and they are right.

I went to Edinburgh and Glasgow to see repertory performances of a play that had been made out of *The Happy Prisoner*, about the man with the amputated leg. It was not a very good play, but it was popular with small companies, because it had only one set and a lot of parts for women.

Coming back from Glasgow after the first night of the play,

I found a seat by the window of the small plane, and was glad that no one came to sit by me. I was tired. I felt frowsty, with hair that had come unstuck and a navy blue suit with a shiny skirt. I wanted to read and sleep.

We were late taking off. A last-minute passenger came on, and people turned to glare at him, as if he were responsible for the delay. The only seat left was next to me. He was an American naval officer. He wanted to talk, to know where I came from – baffling question to an English person – what was the population of the towns we flew over, and whether this or that curious fact he read in his newspaper was true.

I answered in grunts. It was not until we had landed and he stood up, that I took a proper look at him and was inspired to ask if I could drive him to London.

When I went into 52 one afternoon and told them about my American, Henry and Fanny had not met him. I had lived in this family long enough to learn to keep quiet about new love affairs, which tended to get talked to death by speculators.

'I wonder what she sees in him.'

'An American. That Canadian of Cissy's was *most* unstable.'

'Well, let's hope this one lasts longer than some of the others.'

'I always thought it was a pity she didn't marry that nice quiet man in the City.'

'So Hal and Fanny have finally got Monty off the shelf.'

'I'm going to marry an American.'

'Where is he?' Fanny peered eagerly out of the front door, where she had hurried to meet me, as she always did when I came home.

'He's coming later.'

Doady had given me one piece of advice. 'When you take him to 52, wait till Henry's had his dinner, so he won't have that on his mind.'

And I remembered when the news came that my brother had died of malaria in the Mediterranean. Fifty-two was full of family who had come to weep, and Henry wandered about in his slippers in a state of shock, saying, 'Why is dinner so late?'

When I took Roy to Chepstow Villas later that evening, Henry and Fanny, so loving and eager to be nice, had obviously worried more about what he would think of them than they of him. But Henry, as if he expected a ten gallon hat and holsters, had dressed himself up in his old Trinity Hall blazer with the frayed silver crescent on the pocket, and his M.C.C. tie, faded with the suns of Italy and stained with pipe ash and the soups of the Pavilion at Lord's.

'An *American*?' people said who had not met him.

'You're going to live in *America*? O-o-oh,' on a falling note. 'I don't know how you can. Life is so fast there. They have brittle values.'

'Watch out for the martinis.'

'Why can't he come and live in England?'

Some of my friends who had left me behind by marrying at the usual age were already divorced. Now they had lost me a second time. I was still in the wrong camp.

Leaving Hinxworth was very hard. The fact that I was able to showed me that I was sure. Although we had made arrangements for the children to keep their ponies somewhere else, taking the cottage away from them seemed like betrayal. If someone had taken the Oxfordshire cottage away from me at that age . . .

To quiet the guilt, I had to summon the alternative, the nuisance old aunt image. 'She was so good to you when you were young' would be even worse if it was, 'She gave up so much for you.'

By the time I left the village, I was quite involved in local affairs. Unable to keep accounts, I was treasurer of the annual Ashwell Horse Show. I was also President of the Hinxworth Cricket Club, because when I got my advance for *Flowers on the Grass*, I had bought maroon blazers for all the team and the umpire and Mr Brownfield at the pub, who was the Secretary.

Every summer, my own team came from London, a swiping collection of ballet dancers, writers, cousins, middle-aged friends of Henry's and small boys in enormous pads. The village always won, and the day ended in the Three Horseshoes.

Roy's first experience of English village life was sitting in a car (it was too wet for deck chairs), watching my friends from London and Hinxworth play cricket in between spasms of rain.

His second experience was the Ashwell Horse Show, where it rained all day in solid sheets, but that does not stop a horse show. He spent the morning in the Secretary's tent, trying to straighten out my confusion of entry and prize money. A dressage exhibition was performed in the rain. Behind the delicate, neat-stepping horse as it circled the ring went four sodden small girls with seaweed hair, holding a horse rug for people to throw pennies into. Roy spent the afternoon in the tent, counting slippery wet pennies which the small girls with the horse rug poured out on to the trodden grass.

After clearing up the muddle of programme advertising fees, he went back to America, and I took the carrier bags of pennies to the bank in Baldock. The pennies were still wet. As I put the brown paper bags on the counter, the bottoms fell out and the wet pennies spilled all over the bank like cheap largesse. The manager stayed behind the grille. A customer helped me pick up the pennies and count them again, but some of them had rolled under the radiators and may be there still.

For tax reasons, before I left England I had to sell my cottage with the apricot walls and the wide fireplace and the hollyhocks looking into the bathroom. It was still too far for weekenders, and difficult to sell. Only one couple came to see it, while I was packing up to leave. The place was looking its worst, filthy, littered with cardboard boxes and overflowing dustbins, dead flowers, a wet dog and a sink full of dirty plates. It had rained for four days and the garden was a marsh.

The couple went round sniffing and saying, 'Of course there would have to be a lot of things done before we could live *here*,'

143

and peered at me curiously to see who was this woman who could.

Eventually I sold it just before I left for America. I had paid £4,500 for it in 1947. I sold it in 1951 for £1,100. In 1976, I saw it advertised in a London newspaper for £37,000.

14

America was so ugly. That was upsetting at first. The introduction to England from Heathrow to London is not picturesque, but the drive south from the New York docks, through the Lincoln tunnel, past the dumps of Secaucus to the New Jersey Turnpike is shocking.

Dismayed, terrified of marriage after so long an independence, I sat clenching the seat of the car and thinking, *ugly*, *ugly*, *ugly*, as if the word could make any impression on that deliberately hideous landscape of dumps, oil tanks, scrap heaps, and elevated roads conquering the sour marshes on stilted metal legs.

An ageing G.I. bride, I may have been the most insular Englishwoman who ever ventured, for love, into the New World.

At my wedding the next day, in Princeton, New Jersey, I did not know anybody except Roy and four friends of Henry and Fanny's. The church would not let us be married in the sanctuary, because Roy was not a Roman Catholic. We were married in a small vestry room with flowered wallpaper, a *Woman's Own* photographer, and the priest's second best cassock hanging on a nail.

What does it matter? Weddings are wasted on the bride and groom. They are in a coma throughout, and remember almost nothing, except that they could think of better ways to spend the money.

In Washington, we lived on the hill of Georgetown, which was old and charming, with red-brick pavements, and might have been Chelsea, except that the houses were made of wood. Our house in Volta Place was only one room wide, a mere helping of a house, like a slice of pound cake. There was an alley with chic dwellings on one side, and on the other, a junk yard, where I made my first black friends.

The countryside was reassuring, because Maryland and Virginia were green and rolling and wooded, and might have been England, except that it went on for much longer.

I wasted a lot of time comparing, looking for things that were like England, and criticizing things that were not. I wasted a lot of energy arguing about pronunciation and the choice of words. I wasted a lot of emotion being home-sick.

When I found out how to get about the city on buses and street cars, I felt more at home. I went to museums and cinemas and department stores, and bought things I did not need, as if I were on holiday. I saw food in the shops that I had not seen for years. I bought ravenously, on the wartime principle that if you saw something like tinned tongue on a shelf, you bought it whether you wanted it or not, because it might never appear again.

I had never been a housewife before, with a husband leaving and returning on schedule. I listened to all the afternoon soap operas on the radio, and was especially vulnerable to the novelty of commercials. I bought three different kinds of floor wax, although our kitchen only had about thirty square feet of floor. I bought an expensive vacuum cleaner, because when the man came to demonstrate the advertised cheap one, he had stuffed a wad of paper in the hose, so that he could say confidingly, 'This hunk of junk doesn't really suck, but I have a better model in the car . . .'

I washed and ironed Roy's shirts and polished his shoes and cleaned the silver once a week, to show that English women made the best wives. I refused to use the dishwasher, because any woman who could not do her own washing up, etc., etc.

I could not yet get any money out of England. I discovered that American banks do not allow overdrafts. I tried to get a job as a dentist's receptionist and discovered that I had not got the right kind of visa. I tried to sell an article to the magazine section of a Sunday paper, and discovered that they did not want me. When we went out, if I was introduced as a writer, or author-ess, no one had ever heard of me. A woman with Christmas tree earrings said, 'Monica Dickens? How innaresting. So tell me, Miss Dickens, what name do you write under?'

I must have been very conceited and spoiled. I minded. I felt lost and rootless and unwanted. Adjusting to marriage is difficult enough, especially when you are thirty-six. Trying to do it in a strange country was precarious.

Roy was at work all day. As we sweated into one of Washington's intolerable clammy summers, where you are wet again with sweat before you can dry off after a cold shower, I remembered, at last, what I was supposed to be doing, and began to write a book.

I thought, if marriage in Washington was so difficult, even with a husband who was kind and understanding and fun to be with, what would it be like if the man was stuffy and self-centred, and you should never have married him anyway?

The title for that story came from Stevenson's depressing remark that 'Times are changed with him who marries; there are no more bypath meadows where you may innocently linger, but the road lies long and straight and dusty to the grave.'

It helped, being back at my old job. Even the life of a naval officer's wife became more bearable, because it could be observed and chronicled, instead of merely suffered.

The social life of the Washington Navy in the early nineteen fifties was a curio of left-over customs, long ago abandoned by the British.

People still paid calls. One could be contentedly writing, or painting a ceiling, or in bed on a Sunday afternoon. There would be a knock at the door of 3326 Volta Place, and there stood a Captain and his wife, dressed to the hilt, with gloves, arriving unannounced to pay a call, as if they expected to find you sitting, like your grandmother, with nothing else to do but 'receive', with the kettle on the boil and the silver tea service polished.

Worse, much worse, death to a British soul, I was expected to pay calls on senior officers' wives.

'I won't.'

'You must.'

'Does our income depend on it?'

'It's what people *do*.'

'I know what to do, but it's not the same as what *they* do.'

Transatlantic marriages are desirable, but not easy. When you criticize a country's custom, the other person gets defensive, even if they agree. It takes about five years for this foolishness to wear off.

In the articles I wrote for *Woman's Own* long before I was married, telling people how to keep their man happy, I used to remind the women who expected to see me in the greengrocer's that it was a good idea if the wife compromised, and gave up a few unimportant things, so that she could hold out, if necessary, on the fundamentals. I also said that if head-on opposition does not work, you go round the sides.

I tried this out. When ordered to call on some woman who did not want to see me any more than I wanted to see her, I used to telephone her. If someone answered, I would hang up. When the telephone rang and rang without an answer, I jumped in the car, dashed round to the house, shoved my visiting cards through the mail slot with a genteel scrawl, 'So sorry to miss you', and the call was made.

Better for me. Much better for her, except that the hang-up telephone calls may have made her nervous about burglars.

Many of the Washington wives laboured under the illusion that what they did affected their husbands' careers. Perhaps it did. One of the major tortures was the luncheon of the Officers' Wives Club. Some of the younger ones spent money they could not afford on pastel outfits and costume jewellery, and had their hair done in a hard, unbecoming manner and bought a hat to put on top of that. They hired a baby sitter, and drove their husbands to the office, so that they could have the car.

Defying my advice in *Woman's Own*, I refused to go to the lunches at first. Then one of the Admirals' wives, a raddled trouper whom I really liked, begged me to join them, and I saw tears in her jowelled eyes. Perhaps the only way she could sustain belief in the barbarous rituals was if nobody opposed them.

So I did go. It was worse than I feared. I was the only one who was not wearing a hat, and the zip fastener at the back of my dress was undone. All the newcomers were made to stand up and remain standing until they were introduced. My name being Stratton, I stood for a long time. When you were introduced – 'This is Mrs Burgemeier, and she's a *bride!*' – two hundred pairs of eyes, which were individually kindly, amused, indifferent, but en masse were like a phalanx of spears, focused on the part of you above the table to see if you were pregnant.

Many of the brides were. I was not. I was at least ten years older than any of them, and they probably thought I was past it. We ate creamed chicken and peas in patty shells, jello salad and soft sweet rolls, and drank several cups of bitter lukewarm coffee. The Vice-President showed slides of her trip to Ancient Greece, and the Director of the Dee Cee Charm School showed us how to lock the hips and raise the bust.

When Roy came home, I cried too, like the Admiral's wife, though for different reasons. But I suppose one of them – dread of rejection – was the same.

Cocktail parties were not so bad, because you did not go alone, but they were interchangeable. In the Navy, you stick with your own group. We were in the Bureau of Supplies and Accounts. We always saw the same people at all the parties, and had to invite the same people to the parties we gave. There was always a turkey at one end of the buffet table and a ham at the other. I thought that was marvellous at first, and fell on them, until I found that they appeared at every party. Cravenly, when we had to entertain, I discarded my brilliant British ideas about sausage rolls and Scotch eggs and cheese straws, and put a turkey at one end of the table and a ham at the other.

My ham was underdone and my turkey was overdone. I did not cook as well as the capable American wives. I did not manage as well. When I had people to dinner, I flustered in and out of the kitchen with a red face, and wanted to start washing up as soon as I had served the coffee. Poised and gracious American women, who did not go near the kitchen until the third martini, produced incredible things like Beef Wellington without appearing to have actually cooked it.

Once one of these clever little hostesses confided in me after dinner that she cleaned her house for three days before a party, and turned out the cupboards in the children's rooms. Her husband was at a crucial stage in his career. They had done a lot of entertaining. She told me, sitting in her strawberry ice cream bedroom, with immaculate make up and hair and a dress that was cleaned every time she wore it, that she felt she was on the edge of a nervous breakdown.

Roy had been in the Navy since he was sixteen, when he had run away from home and lied about his age to enlist, and he had been thinking about an early retirement. When *No More Meadows* was published, and the Washington wives hated the book, it seemed like a good time to retire.

In case the women at the luncheon had been right, and I was too old to get pregnant, we had decided to adopt a child. American agencies would not even interview us. We were too old, of different religions, and Roy was in the Navy, which was considered unstable. We went to England, and found a baby girl. She was in the kitchen of a crowded foster home, sitting on the floor sucking a dirty crust of bread.

They say that when you see your new-born baby, your whole being reaches out in recognition. That was the way I felt about the fat, grubby child waiting for me among the grime and old food under the kitchen table.

15

We went to live in the New England village of North Falmouth, on Cape Cod. This narrow piece of land, sticking out into the Atlantic south of Boston, is a relic of the terminal moraine of a glacier which crept down from Labrador six hundred thousand years ago and melted, leaving Cape Cod above water, and a few last outcrops which are Martha's Vineyard, Nantucket and the Elizabeth Islands.

The Cape is a curve of sandbar, shaped like a raised arm, with Provincetown as the clenched fist, Chatham the elbow, and Buzzard's Bay, where North Falmouth is, the armpit. It is one of the loveliest places in America, always warmer than the mainland in winter and cooler in summer, and surrounded by incomparable beaches and dunes and marshy inlets. Nothing happens in the winter, but in the summer people swarm over the two bridges of the canal that makes Cape Cod an island.

North Falmouth, where we still live, has no bars or big motels or famous beaches where maniacs in dune buggies are allowed to roar up and down, crushing small tidal life and scattering the gulls. It is the least spoiled village in this tourist paradise. No one comes here, unless they are looking for it. Cars on the highway pass it by, speeding to get somewhere else.

The summer people who come have houses here, and an equal interest in keeping the village unfashionable. The year-round people are builders, plumbers, teachers, and scientists from the marine laboratories at Woods Hole. The houses are of white or weathered wood. Main Street runs through a tunnel of elms. No one here is rich or social. Everyone is sociable when you want to be gregarious, but agreeable when you want to be left alone.

Our house on Main Street, which was built in 1812 for a sea captain, looks quite narrow and puritanical from the front, but it runs back a long way, with all the rooms leading into each other, and most of them facing south. The sun pours in all day and then moves round to set the western windows on fire before it drops into Buzzard's Bay.

When we came here with Pam in 1953, I thought that now I had a baby, I would settle down to be a full time mother, and give up what a man I might have married called 'this writing nonsense', which was why I did not marry him. But the long empty spaces of winter in North Falmouth cried out to be filled with work, and there was something I wanted to write about.

Just before we left London, there had been a visit of some lesser foreign ruler, who was honoured with a small procession through the streets. As I was hurrying round buying things for Pam and arranging for the shipping of furniture, I had wondered about the people who had time to stand on street corners in the middle of the day to wait for somebody to go by who meant nothing to them, of whom perhaps they would never have heard, if the *Daily Express* had not told them to go out and stand on street corners to see him go by.

I wrote a book about a woman who, alas, had time to kill by standing on street corners to see someone go by. I had to re-arrange my writing time, getting up about four and writing until Pam woke. I used to put her to bed as late as possible.

I had never lived in a place where storms came off the sea. That winter, the wind blew the pine trees and old elms outside my writing room unmercifully. Laundry was torn out of your hands before you could peg it to the line. The back door blew open and the cat blew in with it, half across the kitchen. The storms came up from nowhere. As the wind began, the bare trees and bushes danced as if they were glad to feel the motion. Hours later, when they had been pushed and shaken and tormented too long, they were like exhausted children, moving their petulant heads from side to side, 'Oh, leave us alone!'

I called the book *The Winds of Heaven*, because the drifting life of the woman in it was being blown this way, that way, and not left alone.

When Pam was about two and a half, we went back to England to find another daughter.

We were taken to a children's home on the south coast to see a little girl who was fat and blonde and jolly like Pam, above the waist, but dwindled into weak legs and feet. She had been passed by an orthopaedic surgeon, but if you held her to stand with her feet on the ground, she was not jolly any more. She cried.

Perhaps adopted children ought to be chosen as carefully as you wish they were able to choose you. But there is no choice. You are so delighted to be offered a baby that you grab the first one. I expected to do that with this child. Going to see her had seemed like the last step, not the first. In anticipation, she was already ours. I was not prepared for indecision.

Better people than us would have taken her willingly, hoping either that she would develop normally, or that they would be able to cope if she did not. I hope that our decision not to adopt her was not only cowardice, but an awareness that we were not the right parents to cope.

Having admitted that we did not take the little girl with weak legs because we did not want to risk a handicapped child, I will offer the justification that if we had taken her, we would not have got Prudence.

When we told the social worker that we were not sure about the child, she said, 'Well, it's all there is.'

'Do you mean that if we don't take her, we may not get a child?'

'Who knows? You're not top priority.'

We agonized, driving back in her car. Coming into London, she said, 'I've just thought. There is a baby who's just come available. She's been fostered ever since she was born.'

'What's she like?' It hardly mattered.

'Odd little thing. You may not –'

'Let's go and see her.'

The odd little thing had no hair and was being carried about a suffocating small house on the hip of a large motherly woman. If she was put down, she tottered, with lifted hands, and went, 'Up, up.' She was umbilically attached to her foster mother. The only other person she would look at was jolly old Pam. When

Pam got off my knee and approached her with her squared off, rolling boxer's walk, the baby laughed, and for the first time you could see her as an independent human being.

'Is this the one?'

Pam nodded. 'This one.'

Bringing up adopted children is exactly like bringing up your own, and yet not like.

To the love and belonging, it makes no difference whether you have given birth, or found them under a kitchen table, or on the wide hip of a foster parent. Mothers and their growing children do not love each other because one was inside the other for nine months, but because of what has been shared since birth.

Diligently, you tell the adopted child the right supportive things – 'This is *your* family', without making them feel rejected by their first one.

'Your mother and father were not living together. They wanted you to have a proper family life. It was very unselfish of them.'

'We chose you. You are special. Other parents have to take what they get. We chose *you*.'

Then they work it out for themselves.

Pam said, 'God gave me to the wrong woman first.'

Diana, my niece Mary's daughter, digested the ego-building stories. Later she said quite contentedly, 'Nobody didn't want me before you and Daddy.'

Even though no secret is made of the adoption, it hardly ever comes up. Everyone forgets it. The children grow a bit like you because they copy expressions and mannerisms, or people see a resemblance because they expect it.

'Pammie's like her Mummy, and Prudy is like her Daddy. Oh my.'

The joys and rewards are the same as with a natural child. The difficulties and pains are the same, with one extra. There are conflicts, especially the compulsive one between the adolescent fighting for independence and the parents fighting for control, which leave no winners. For the adoptive parents, the sense of failure bears the added anxiety of wondering whether somebody else might have done a better job.

People say – not to the child's face, thank God – 'What a lucky little girl . . .' But if you had not adopted her, someone else would have. There were plenty of people in line, and she might have had a better deal. She might have found a family whose basic beliefs and instincts more nearly matched the ones she inherited.

As time goes on, you change your ideas about the balance of influence between heredity and environment. Adoption is not easy . . . for the child.

North Falmouth is a very fine place to bring up children. There is just enough snow and skating in the winter, and such a long summer of swimming and doing things in little boats that by the end of August they are sated with the beach, and grumbling, 'There's nothing to do in this place.'

Cape Cod doctors make a good living out of all the retired people, but they don't make much out of the children. They hardly ever get colds. This stretch of western coast between the canal and Woods Hole is especially healthy. Some of the old families who still own the great grey houses with their Victorian porches and pinnacles originally came here because they had a sickly child who would not thrive anywhere else.

It is also a good place to see anybody you ever knew, because if you live by the sea in a climate like this, everybody comes to visit you.

Henry and Fanny transferred their regular Hinxworth visits across the Atlantic, and came every summer. They always came by boat, even after flying became safe and comfortable. They always came by Cunard, because – well, because it was Cunard. They always came on one of the smaller Cunarders, like the *Parthia* and the *Scythia*, because they knew all the crew. They had the same cabin with the same stewardess, whose life history and family problems were meat and drink to Fanny, and the barman had Henry's martini ready at noon and six, just as he appeared in the doorway of the smoking room.

I would meet them in New York, and we would take the Cape

155

Codder from Grand Central station, past the tenements of Harlem, through Bridgeport and Westport, over the thrilling Connecticut river at Old Saybrook, through Providence to the land of wine-coloured cranberry bogs, and across the Cape Cod canal by the drawbridge, right into North Falmouth.

By this time the train was reduced to one carriage, a parlour car of armchairs and little tables for your drink and sandwich and a smiling porter to bring them. If Henry had designed the whole trip, from the boat train Pullman at Waterloo, it could not have suited them better.

When train service to Cape Cod was discontinued, and the little North Falmouth station burned down by vandals, I drove my parents up from New York. The long journey, like the short one from London to Hinxworth, was interrupted by ritual stops at certain places and certain times of day.

Henry wore a wristwatch, and also a chain across his waistcoat with his gold watch at one end and his penknife for piercing cigars and sharpening crossword puzzle pencils at the other. The watches were used for different purposes. For any old consultation, like the answer to, 'What's the time, Gramps?' he would raise his hand, shake it like a thermometer and look at his wristwatch. For a regular checking of the stable things of life, the gold watch was drawn out of his waistcoat pocket and held in front of him in the palm of his hand.

Driving in America, long distance, or just to Boston, or the end of the Cape, Henry would stir in the passenger seat about noon, humph a little, then pull out the gold watch and look at it in some surprise, although he knew what the time was, which was why he had pulled it out.

'Well, well. Almost time for a little drink.'

Shades of the A1 from London to Hinxworth, except that the Connecticut Turnpike between New York and Massachusetts does not have the Comet or the George and Dragon. Drinks are not available in any highway restaurants. We would have to get off the road and search for a place that served both drinks and edible food, because I was in no mood to go through the whole search again for lunch.

If the aunts, God bless them, were alive to object to this book – 'It's in rather bad taste' – they might complain that I make my father sound like an alcoholic. He was not. Henry loved good wine, and he liked a gin at certain times of day. It is impossible to write about him without the rituals and traditions that sustained his grasp on life, and gin was one of the rituals.

In North Falmouth, he wore his old white tennis flannels, let out with a gusset of a slightly different shade in the back seam, and the shapeless panama hat that I had holidayed with in Lenno and Fasano and Pontresina and Calvi and Sorrento and Dubrovnik and Albania. Every morning he walked to the post office to get his airmail *Times*, and every afternoon after his sleep in a long chair under the trees he would stroll round the village. He made a lot of contacts on his walks, not only with people working in their gardens, but with the drivers who stopped to offer him a lift, not believing that he could be out walking for pleasure.

Americans are marvellous to old people, taking special care to fuss over them and make them welcome. Henry and Fanny, who had mourned Hinxworth but never said so, lest it made me feel bad about marrying abroad, recovered their visiting pleasure.

People loved them. They loved it that Henry grew increasingly like one of his grandfather's characters, and that they were both so English that they could not always be understood. Henry was taken to the county courthouse to be venerated as a megalith of British Law, and Fanny held groups of women enthralled with comic dissertations on the servant problem, even though they had little conception of what she was talking about.

We went back to London almost every year, to get the information I needed for the novels that I was still writing about England.

The Angel in the Corner was again about a woman who married an impossible man. I seem to have been obsessed with

157

that, as if I could not believe my own luck. *Man Overboard* was about the man who gets off the bus on impulse, only this time he got off a train to confront the woman he kept seeing in a garden.

When I first went back to England, television and newspaper interviewers behaved as if I had returned from the jungle. They wanted me to say comical things about the Americans, as if I had been there as an amused anthropologist, instead of a resident. In the days before commonplace transatlantic air travel, the Americans were people in films, an alien 'they', like freakish animals in a zoo.

The first time we all went back to London, Henry was ill, so we took the girls to a flat opposite the public lavatories in the street that ends with the Paddington Baths, nostalgic temple where Charles Pick had said to me twenty years earlier, 'You ought to write a book.'

It was a terrible little dump, but it was the only affordable place we could find, spoiled Americans that we were, with proper heat.

There was only one bedroom, where the girls slept on one bed and a chair with an end that pulled groggily out and would have collapsed if Prudence had been heavier. The kitchen was small and disgusting. In the living room, the carpet was so old, it came up in dusty shreds if you vacuumed. Perhaps that was why there was no vacuum cleaner, and I had to borrow Mrs Catchpole's erratic sucker from 52. The short bath was always full of filthy children or their clothes, since the only place for them to play was in a sooty yard at the back and a narrow court at the front, which had a dip in it that was always filled with black rain water. Roy and I slept on a disappearing bed that stood on its head in a cupboard in the living room. When it was down, it blocked the front door, and nobody could get in or out.

We drove about in Henry's blue Vauxhall which was still functioning, its bumpers more wildly curled than ever. Henry was involved in a feud with an embittered man who kept a barrow in the garage opposite his in the mews behind 52. It was not like his war with the Italian and the oil paintings of big-headed children. That had been love-hate, but this was all hate on both sides. The barrow man, to whom Henry was a capitalist, because he had a battered car with curly bumpers and a loose exhaust, would leave his barrow outside, making it almost impossible for Henry to turn into his garage. From behind their grimy top window, the man and his wife would watch with sullen triumph the splintering of doorposts and torturing of metal. The side mirror went, and once when I was parking the car, a door handle was torn off.

The next time we came to London we stayed at 52, and a gentle girl came every day to teach the girls. They spent most of the lessons lying on the rug in front of the popping gas fire, kicking their heels and pretending not to understand English. The gentle tutor's reports used to read, 'Went down to get biscuits from Mary Vinton' – Mrs Catchpole's successor – 'and never came back.' 'Spent forty minutes sulking in top lav.' 'Stated she wished I had never been borned.'

On our next visit, in the cruelly cold winter of 1963, Pam and Prudy, in English school uniforms that did not make them look English, went to the convent school in Chepstow Villas that gave them the holy pictures they peddled in the Portobello Road market.

16

This south-eastern part of Massachusetts is not blanketed with snow all winter, like the northern states of New England. The snow comes and goes, at first a delight, transforming the landscape, usually disappearing before it gets boring. It falls again, to lie about the Boston streets in blackening lumps which melt in a rush on a freak warm day and flood the subway and people's cellars. The ground freezes and thaws, freezes and thaws. The roads buckle into bumps and potholes, and roses have a hard time surviving.

At least twice each winter, the jolly television men in blazers who announce the weather as proudly as if they had invented it, give us heavy, knock-out blizzards. The highway from Cape Cod to Boston becomes a nightmare wasteland, littered with overturned trucks and abandoned cars, as if people had been overtaken by the end of the world. But the snow ploughs are out before the storm ends. They have the roads open within a few hours, and the routine of commuting goes blindly on, with the slush from cars ahead freezing on the windscreen.

In 1946, when there was two feet of snow in north Hertfordshire, life came to a total halt for three days, and the village of Hinxworth was saved by Mr Brownfield from the Three Horseshoes riding a farm horse through the drifts to Ashwell and coming back with a sack of bread, a hero.

In 1953, our first Christmas in North Falmouth, I pulled Pam down the hill on a sled over the packed snow to get a present from the Know Your Neighbor Club, dispensing neighbourliness outside the crossroads drug store, where a boy played carols on a gramophone from the back of an open van. Now more than twenty years later, there are too many children for the Know Your Neighbor Club to know, and too many carols have already been piped for too many weeks into shopping centres and office lifts and aeroplanes, and not only the dentist's waiting room, but the very chamber where you recline agape.

Cameron came down the empty white street on his old brown horse, dressed as Santa Claus. There was a package with my child's name on it. I felt for the first time that I belonged in this small discreet place. Village people had been agreeable, reserving judgement. Some of them had made a point of telling me about the other Englishwoman who once lived in our house, who had flown the Union Jack on the fourth of July.

Since all my history teachers had claimed that England never lost a war, they had to leave out the American Revolution, or be caught lying. I was not sure what the fourth of July signified, except a warning not to be too British. But now with the old sled called Flexible Flyer I had found in the cellar, and Pam's red snow suit and my plaid wool jacket, I felt that I qualified as a local mother, and was happy about that.

Winters are much colder here than in England, and yet warmer, because the sun shines most of the time in an intense blue sky, clothes are thicker, and you can stand being out in lower temperatures if you know you can be warm indoors.

When I remember unbearable cold, I am thinking about English winters. The Sussex house, where Mrs Hampden tried to freeze out her tubercle bacillus in the garden shed, and the baby and I bawled together as I fumbled to dress her in the kitchen with the fire gone out. A dinner party before a hunt ball at a country house in Yorkshire – the masochism of that social life – where I was either too vain or too shy to go upstairs and put on a cardigan over my sleeveless taffeta. Monday mornings at Sunbeam Talbot, where your fingers stuck to the gear wheels. A hotel in Bournemouth where the bathroom window was fixed to stay open. A house in Berkshire where I lay in bed in coat, gloves and boots and watched the curtains billowing inwards from the closed window.

I think about that terrible English winter of 1963, when people died of cold, and filthy lumps of ice like cast iron stayed in the middle of Oxford Street for weeks, with the buses bumping over them. Fanny sat at dinner with a hot water bottle in her lap, and we stuffed cotton wool round the edges of the high Georgian windows of 52.

I was going round with case workers from the N.S.P.C.C. The things that I needed to see I saw at their worst in that long cruel winter.

'Are you writing anything now?' A casual question at a party from my cousin who was an M.P.

'I've just finished a book about cruelty to animals.'

'Oh look.' He stopped smiling. 'You should be writing about cruelty to children. We're getting shocking reports.'

'I don't know that I . . .'

When someone tells you what you should write, or wear, or do to your hair, your first reaction is defence against implied criticism. Later, you may get round to it as your own idea. My cousin, having planted his seed, passed on like a transient father and left me germinating.

It was in the middle of that ironclad winter, when old people gave up and ill-shod children got frostbite, that I started going round with inspectors and case workers from the National Society for the Prevention of Cruelty to Children. The Americans have changed the name to Children's Protective Services, but the British name stays, and the inspector is still called amiably 'the cruelty man' in neighbourhoods where he is known.

These people were invincible. I was ready to die of cold and exhaustion halfway through each afternoon, but there was always one more wretched house to visit, one more reported family to track down at the top of five flights of stairs.

The inspectors were married. Their wives often had to take in for the night a child removed in an emergency. Sometimes they found a mewing bundle on their doorstep. Miss Zils, the fiery, wiry case worker in South London was against marriage for herself.

'When I get home from a day like this, the last thing I want to see is a husband.'

As we went round her beat in her draughty little car, lurching over the ice lumps day after bitter day, we heard about husbands. They desert you. They beat you. They knock you up again even before the stitches from the last birth are out. They drink your rent money. They wear you down with brutishness. It is not all the man's fault. The abuse has too many complicated and backward-reaching causes to be any one person's fault. It is not the mother's fault, except for inviting brutality, the way some women unconsciously do, and for continuing to bear child after child until she is little more than a hollowed shell, scoured of all sap and hope.

'I knew a cat,' said the matron of a day nursery on the last uphill gasps of Notting Hill, a healthy girl with the sleeves of her blue overall rolled over strong hairy arms. 'Even a cat – she was dried out, exhausted, killed by giving birth. And cats don't have brutal, selfish husbands.'

The woman whose child we had come to see sat on a bench in the corridor, large head tied up in a scarf, ankle socks on mottled legs.

'I done the best I can,' she repeated, not as an excuse, but as something to say. 'I done what I can.'

Her three-year-old boy had been found last month with a bruised back and a long burn on his leg that looked as if it was made with a poker.

'When my husband come out of stir,' the woman said, 'and saw the burn on Gregory, he hit me in the stomach with a piece of wood – I was carrying. Not his. "You done it, you dirty cow," he said.'

'Did you?' the inspector asked, not accusingly.

'I done what I can.'

Today the child had arrived at the nursery with bruises on his balding head and peaky face.

'He fell on concrete.'

'The bruises are on the *top* of his head.'

'His brother done it.'

When the matron brought the little wobbly boy out to her, he screamed and ran back into the nursery.

Outside in the wind that swung up Ladbroke Grove like a

mailed fist, a baby lay in a pram with a bandaged head and nostrils full of blood. A fractured skull?

'It's his ears,' the mother said, and wheeled him off downhill with her face flattened back by the wind, leaving the three-year-old for the doctor, who had to be called before a child could be removed to safety.

In that Notting Hill area, in whose lower reaches I had been born and brought up, and through which I had bicycled for a year to the aircraft factory, I followed Mr Bowes, who knew it better, and knew different bits of it. In a tall brick house near Rillington Place, renamed Ruston Close after John Reginald Christie filled No. 10 with female corpses, a borough official had once managed to count fifty-six residents. There may have been more. They were never all home at once. The beds were used in shifts.

In a room at the top of this teeming building, which harboured music and laughter and West Indian cooking smells as well as sour misery, we found a sick baby, not so much asleep as in a sort of coma, bundled in a stiff blanket in the corner of a greasy leather sofa, the only furniture in the room. There was no water or heat, nothing to cook on, nowhere to put anything. A suitcase without a lid was piled with clothes and broken shoes. Opened tins, the end of a loaf, a cup of milk, a bowl of half-eaten food stood on the floor.

'She is out.' A very small Turkish man with trousers cut off raggedly round his feet came out of a triangular closet by the stairs. He was making tea. The closet, which was his home, was thick with steam, like a Turkish bath.

'Does she often leave the baby alone?' Mr Bowes asked.

'I don't know.'

'Someone reported it.'

'What? What is?' The small man became unable to understand English.

The baby woke and cried like a reed. It vomited up some watery fluid. It looked yellow and waxy, like floor soap. When it went on crying, a girl came up from below with a huge red furious baby on her hip.

'I'll take him down with mine.'

Mr Bowes went to telephone, so I went down to her room, which was warmer. It had a little basin, and had obviously been a bedroom in what was once a Victorian family house with servants lugging coal and jugs of hot water up the flights of stairs. There were two other small children, staggering about with no clothes below the waist. The huge baby had none either.

'Saves washing.' The girl was pregnant again, although she only looked about fifteen.

I sat on the floor and held the sick smelly baby from upstairs, until a hollow-eyed blonde pulled open the door.

'Where's my baby?' I got up and she took the bundle from me. 'Who are you?'

'I came with Mr Bowes.'

'The cruelty man? He's not going to take my baby away!'

I heard that many times, the authorities seen as kidnappers, but actually the rights of parents are very carefully protected.

But being 'put away' is the age-old bogey of lunatics locked up for ever in asylums, children wrenched from their mother's bosom into institutions, never to be seen again.

'I'm not going to have him put away!' cries the exhausted woman whose whiny, 'dirty' boy has been the last straw that toppled her precarious control and makes her chuck him against the table leg, or hold his hand over the burner.

And if the child is removed to a foster home, where there is food and warmth and security, he will be content for a couple of weeks and then want to know, 'When am I goin' 'ome?'

The fifteen-year-old's husband, a mental defective of about forty, came home, so I went upstairs with the hollow-eyed blonde and sat on the blackened sofa and tried not to shiver, while she told me things about her life and times. I wanted to put my arms round her, for warmth as well as sorrow, but this was at the beginning of my time with the N.S.P.C.C., and I was afraid of being resented.

Miss Zils had told me, 'No one will mind. You'll see. When I ask a question, they will answer to you. A new pair of ears.'

And so it was. The sagas unrolled. Miss Zils would ask

briskly, 'How is everything?' and the oft-told story would be related once more to me.

There was nothing I could say to help, but I found out that the less you say, the more you can help. As a writer, I had listened to people because I needed to get the story, not because they needed to tell it. In that sad cold winter of discoveries, I found out the value of listening, and how people are starved for it.

It was so cold in many of the places we went to that, even in outdoor clothes, you had to squeeze yourself together to keep from shivering, and set your jaw to stop your teeth chattering when you talked. If I was invited to take off my coat, it seemed insulting not to, as if to say that I was cold made me different from the people who had been cold for so long here that they had stopped saying it.

There I sit, rigid in boots and slacks and layers of sweaters, while the child on my lap wears a torn nylon dress that someone has thought suitable to give to the Salvation Army. She has an elastic tied round her waist with a piece of cloth looped through it for knickers. A toddler with blue marbled legs staggers about with an empty bottle stuck in its mouth, like a contaminated lollipop. There is a baby in the corner in a pram without wheels. All the children have sores round their mouth and nose. In the fireplace, a small electric heater gives a little light, but no heat, since the piles of grey washing on the fireguard make the room a dank cave. Socks hang like stalactites from strings under the ceiling.

There is always washing under the ceiling. There is always a motor bike, or bits of one, in the front yard, or in the hall if there is no front yard. Ten-year-old girls automatically pick up crying babies, so that their hips and stomachs stick out long before their time. Children are pretty because they are children, but their parents are a ravaged preview of what poverty will make of them. Babies sit uncannily still. Black babies sit like dolls, and soak steadily through the soaked mattress.

Inspector Emery took me to an underground flat where three

thin black children sat on a bed in a tiny back room that was ankle-deep in filth. The stove and sink were in the passage. On the way out, while we waited by the door for the mother to find the rent book, Mr Emery quickly opened a door and showed me a large front room with a brass double bed, a dressing table with doilies and a set of brushes, fringed lamps, satin quilt and cushions, and a purple carpet. The whole resplendent room appeared completely unused.

In a council flat I went to with Miss Zils, there was one large room full of bicycles, newspapers, tins and assorted rubbish, while the family of four lived in a tiny room with no furniture except a cocktail cabinet with jugs marked Johnny Walker, and a beaten up zinc bath which was the baby's cot.

Mr Bowes and I penetrated to the end of a cul-de-sac behind the terraces the West Indians had colonized. On the ground floor of a derelict house with the basement dripping and top floor boarded up, a woman whose man had disappeared at the start of winter lived with four wild children, who ran in and out in the freezing rain with their trousers hanging down and the backs of their shoes trodden in. They were all filthy, but every chair was piled with clean clothes. There were blankets washed and folded, but only rags on the beds. In the kitchen, where your heels sank in the clotted dirt and food, there was a tiny sink with a cold tap, where the cheerful, warty, gap-toothed woman did her mountains of washing.

'We had no water last week,' she told Mr Bowes, through me, reaching out to slap a crying child, and kicking another as he raced by. 'I carried buckets through the snow from the end of the road. Caught my death.' Her laugh became a choke, became a visceral cough.

'Perhaps the washing is too much for you ...' Mr Bowes usually made statements as suggestions.

'There's always the wash to be done.' She shook imaginary suds off her thick bare arms.

Though not used. The laundry obsession, like the splendid front room in the subterranean flat, seemed to be a sort of insurance against total defeat.

*

When it was time to start writing the book, I did not want to stop going round with the case workers. I wished that I were one of them. I asked Mr Bowes how he got this job, and why. He had formerly been a sergeant instructor in the Army.

'I'd always lived by the sword,' he said, not looking at me while he drove his little car like a red hot pepper through the North Kensington streets. 'The Bible says, "All they that take the sword shall perish with the sword." I thought that I'd never done anything for other people, except to learn how to kill them, and teach others how to. So I thought – well, people. A lot of what happens to them is their own fault. But children . . .' He looked at me then. When he smiled, his burly soldier's face was sweet and defenceless.

I lived by the pen, and so I must eventually stop looking and listening and go home and shut myself away and make a book of it. I still did not know who my main characters were.

I found one of them in the juvenile court, where I spent a lot of time listening to the magistrates, and the sorry procession of children and adolescents and their parents who come before them.

The children stand in front of the bench, which is only a long table covered with a cloth to conceal the legs of the women magistrates. They stand head up and defiant, or hiding under their hair and muttering. Their eyes are either on the floor, or in a corner of the ceiling, not on the magistrate, whom they do not address as Sir, but sometimes Miss, or Mist. The mother or father or occasionally both stand behind them and say things like, 'I can't do nothing with her,' or, 'He's always been a good boy,' or, 'I can't understand it. If he was short, he'd only to come to me.'

The Etonian magistrate, who is kinder than he looks, always says, 'Give this lady a seat,' even if she is not pregnant, which she often is. The mother sits, hands red from cold, clutching a vast handbag, and tries to put up a front, although she is often so panicky that she can hardly remember her child's name or age. Veterans of the court, appearing yet once more with the same or a different child, exchange domestic details with Miss Younghusband, a charming wise old lady who takes a lot of time, while the other magistrates fidget and wonder about lunch.

And here, among the two small black girls with frightened woolly hair who had been interfered with by the lodger, the boy who stole pennies from a wishing well, the boys who stole bicycles and purses from old ladies, the girl whose mother beat her up when she was pregnant, I found the girl I needed for my story.

Linda had been found in a café with some soldiers. Small, dirty, breastless in a man's shirt and torn jeans, her straw hair teased up and not combed out for days, she stood with her face lifted to keep the tears from spilling over. Her father, square and neckless with a bashed-about face, recited his grievances. 'Uncontrollable . . . two larceny charges previous . . . man-mad . . . my wit's end . . . can't do nothing with 'er . . .'

Linda stood silent, swaying in her broken sandals. When he got to, 'Never comes 'ome when she's told to,' she suddenly let out a wail of anguish that pierced the stuffy mid-afternoon courtroom.

'What is there to come home for!'

On the days when I was not in court, I was still touring the seamier reaches of South London with Miss Zils. She and I were in some pretty harrowing situations that winter, and we became rather close. She was volatile and vulnerable and not at all inured to suffering.

The worst place we went to was the basement of a big Victorian house near the Crystal Palace in Dulwich, the kind of house that Herman Runge had lived in with his growing family.

In what had once been the kitchen of a prosperous merchant's house, a woman called Queenie lived with four children and an intermittent husband who was more trouble than he was worth when he was there. She was christened Queen Mary, Miss Zils told me as we struggled in low gear up a slippery Sydenham hill, because she was born when Queen Mary launched the *Queen Mary*, the last fancy thing her parents did for her.

'She was abused as a child, and her mother before her, I think. Now she's doing it. This is what happens.'

We stumbled down the crippling path to the basement door under the front steps of the empty house, and ducked past a sort of glacier which had formed between a dripping rainpipe and the water butt. Miss Zils banged on the door. We waited, nose drips frozen, feet lifeless. She banged again and shouted angrily. One of the things that endeared her to me was that she was not inhumanly patient.

The door opened a crack, and as we pushed it, the little girl who had opened it fell off the box on which she had stood to reach the handle. She ran ahead of us down a passage like a burrow. Miss Zils tripped over the box, swore, and fumbled for the light switch. Nothing.

'What's this?'

At the end of the passage, we had come into a room fitfully lit by candle ends and a mean coal fire.

'They stole the meter money again.' A thin woman with long black hair draping a chalk white face was nursing a baby in a lopsided armchair by the fire. 'The electric company cut us off.'

'Stole? Who? Where is the meter?' Miss Zils picked up the little girl, who was hanging on to her coat pocket.

'Outside under the steps.'

'Oh my God. Why didn't you tell me?'

'She just has.' On the other side of the fireplace, Queen Mary's brother, an oafish lad of about seventeen sat backwards in the only other chair with his fly open, and endlessly polished the spokes of a bicycle wheel. 'Ha-ha,' he added.

'Why aren't you at work?' Miss Zils was in no mood for ha-ha.

'I left the sweet factory. Got fed up.'

'Too lazy to suck.' Queen Mary put her meagre breast back inside her black dress and got up to put the baby into a drawer which stood on the table. It coughed like a derelict.

'When did the doctor see him last, Queenie?'

'I'm taking him tomorrow.' If she was born the year the *Queen Mary* was launched, she must have been about twenty-seven, but in her old black dress, with her dyed raven hair and gaunt white face, she looked more like fifty.

As Miss Zils discussed practicalities with her, I wandered round the room. It was too cold to sit down. There was nowhere to sit. A large Alsatian dog had jumped into the chair when Queenie got up. That left an iron bed with no mattress or bedding, and another bed with three mattresses piled on it, and a two-year-old perched on top among sodden newspapers. Out of a corner, as I went to that end of the room, came a boy of about seven, with a long bony chin like an old man and hedgehog hair.

'Who are you?' I crouched down to his size, but he backed away into the room, staring.

'It's George.' Miss Zils put her hand in her pocket. 'Here. I brought you a packet of biscuits.'

George took them with a hand like a small claw.

'Last time you give him biscuits, he buried them in the garden,' Queenie's brother said. 'Like the dog when he's got a bone, ha-ha.'

'The ground is too hard to bury them today,' Miss Zils said bravely.

As we drove off to deal with the electric company, she told me about George. He had been taken away three years ago for 'failure to thrive'.

'They stop eating. A sort of suicide. A rejected child can will not to live. But he pined in the hospital and he was worse in a foster home, so we do what we can to keep the family together.'

'Queenie rejects him?'

'His father. He takes no notice of him, even when he's at home. George is a bedwetter, naturally. At Christmas, he stole a little tree, and told me his father bought it.'

All week, in and out of other awful places, as Miss Zils pursued her undaunted pilgrimage, I had George on my mind. When I read about a child left out to get frostbite, and a boy shut up in a chicken coop so long that his legs were curved round the perch, I saw them as George.

When we went back under the glacier, the lights were on.

Queenie's brother sat on the fireguard with his fly open. George was at school. The dog had defecated under the sink.

'Well?' Miss Zils came briskly into the room.

'I got bad news for you,' the brother said lazily. 'The baby died. Friday it was. Bronchitis.'

'Didn't she take him to the doctor?'

'I dunno.'

'You *fools!*' I had never seen her so angry. Her sharp, clever face became very red. I thought she was going to cry. The little girl hung on to her clothes as if she were climbing a fence, but she did not pick her up. 'Where's Queenie?'

'Gone to see about the funeral. Cost thirty pounds, it will.'

'Oh my God.' Useless to suggest the money should be spent on the living. 'What's that?' On the laundry line under the ceiling, a boy's new suit hung next to the dead baby's starched christening robe.

'For Georgie to wear at the funeral.' The brother looked hopeful that Miss Zils would at last be pleased, but she turned and pushed me out of the room and down the passage, with the dog barking behind us.

Weeks later, we went back to that house just before I left London to return to America, in a van from an agency Miss Zils had bullied into giving mattresses and bedding and clothes. She and I dragged the old rancid mattresses out into the back yard and burned them with newspapers from the greenhouse where the little girl and the two-year-old were set to do their job on potties under the broken glass.

The fumes from the mattresses were a stinking smoke signal. George and the little girl, with her trousers round her ankles, came out and danced.

Queenie came out wrapped in a blanket and watched us probing at the mattresses and lighting wads of paper to stuff in the spreading black holes. 'Wouldn't catch me doing that,' she said, 'even if I wasn't carrying.'

'You're *precknant*?' Miss Zils gave the adjective a salivary Rhineland disgust.

'Hope so. Bring the dead one back, see?' Queenie said with a vacant grin, and then shrilly, 'Get in the house, George!'

He went on dancing and yelling.

'He's been in trouble again,' she told me. 'Stole some books from the library. Took them to school and said his Dad bought them for him. What would you do with such a liar?'

George ran into the house. What would I do with him? I wanted to take him away, feed him, teach him, treasure him. Instead, I only took him back in my head and wrote about him.

After the book *Kate and Emma* was published, Miss Zils wrote and told me that she had hoped I had forgotten that she had lost her temper and shouted, 'You fools!' when the baby died. 'Or at least that you wouldn't put it into the book.'

How could I not? It was one of the most touching things about this indomitable woman, that she was not totally armoured against the stupidity and muddle and misery she battled against every day.

17

The next winter, I went with Roy to Australia and New Zealand, where it was summer, to try to sell copies of *Kate and Emma* by sitting in bookshops and signing books.

In 1964, autographing tours had been overdone. Hardly anyone would bother to go round the corner to meet an author. In Australia, however, they had not got many authors of their own, and they did not see many of the European and American authors whose books they bought in gratifying quantities. I had not seen so many people in a bookshop since Helsinki. If they could not buy, they went into the shop in their lunch hour and read a book, chapter by chapter, turning down a page to mark their place for the next day.

Managers did not seem to mind. At least it got people into the shop. As we drove through Melbourne from the airport, I was excited to see crowds of people surging in and out of one of the big bookshops in the middle of the day.

'What's happening?' Perhaps they had come a day early to see me.

'Nothing. It's lunchtime.'

But where were they all the next day when I was sitting at a table exposed to public ridicule, with a pen and piles of my books, trying to look as if I were there for pleasure, rather than commerce?

'If only you hadn't come on a Wednesday!'

The manager, who had spent the last three months corresponding with my publisher about the exact best date and time for the visit, wrung his hands at me reproachfully. 'It's early closing.'

Or late shopping day. Or pensions day. Or the Test Match. Or too near the beginning of the week, or too near the weekend, or raining, or too fine, or any of the other esoteric excuses I have heard in bookshops all over the world.

In England, where I travelled all over the country on an autographing tour for Penguin Books, Jimmy Edwards the radio comedian had just published his autobiography, so 'If only you hadn't come on a Wednesday!' was followed by, 'You should have been here last week when old Jimmy was here. Talk about crowds! We had to get the police out. They had ambulances standing by.'

For an author, brash enough about revealing the inner self, having to peddle the product like a street vendor is humiliating. Wednesday or not, pensions or rain or bus strikes, you know perfectly well that there is only one reason why crowds are not trampling each other to get into the shop.

Nobody cares.

Charitable managers bring out a small pile of books from the back of the shop, and pretend that they have had advance orders for signed copies from people who could not be there. Not challenging the merciful lie, you sign the books with slow penmanship to fill up time. Even if the shop cannot sell them, at least they can't return them to the publishers, with the title page defaced.

I loved New Zealand, with its paradox of uproarious nature and respectable people. I loved Australia. I wanted to live there for two years and be a Melbourne housewife in a new house at the end of a raw unpaved street that crept yard by yard out into the wild as the houses were built. I loved taking a teapot on picnics, and being called Mon by strangers, and calling them Stu and Maur and Gord and Ame, and exchanging terrible relaxed jokes in the first five minutes.

Amidst so much that was different, one thing was very familiar. Into the bookshops of both Australia and New Zealand came the same people I had met in England in my picaresque pursuit of Penguin sales. They fall into a few basic categories, and like the excuses of bookshop managers, are recognizable anywhere in the world.

First there is the woman who picks out a paperback copy of

somebody else's book and brings it to you to wrap and give change.

'I'm sorry. I haven't any paper.'

'No paper! In a shop this size?'

'Well, you see, I'm not actually *selling* books. That is, I'm selling them, but I'm not actually selling them.'

'What are you doing then?' She is staring at a placard which announces that Miss D will autograph copies of her novel *Kate and Emma* this very afternoon.

'I'm, er –' It is quite embarrassing. The manager, who was hovering before, telling you how the shop was torn apart when Kurt Vonnegut was here, is nowhere to be seen. All the assistants seem to have gone to lunch. The publisher's representative is in the pub with Roy. 'I'm, er – supposed to be signing copies of my book.'

'I see.' A tight-lipped nod. *I might have suspected as much.* She takes the paperback and goes balefully away.

Then there are the people who think I am Charles Dickens. They bring me his books to sign. After them come all those who are distantly related to my great-grandfather, or whose great-aunt's cousin's mother's piano teacher once sat on his knee when she was a child.

They come thick and fast in Australia. Two of Dickens's sons, Alfred Tennyson and Edward Bulwer Lytton (all Dickens's sons were named after famous writers) had emigrated here, and although only Alfred had children, and they were two daughters who never married, the country appeared to be half populated with my relations. They flocked into the bookshops, not to buy books and not to meet me, but to let me meet them. 'I knew you'd be so interested.' Sometimes they came looking like Dickens characters, by mistake or on purpose.

Then comes a woman somewhat like a Dickens relation, in that she is dressed in the kind of clothes you don't see in shops. This is no Dickens, however. This is somebody's aunt. She hurries in, breathless with tales about a niece of whom you have never heard.

'Peggy told me to be sure to come and see you, so here I am, though I waited two hours in the rain for the bus, and the doctor dared me to go out and no doubt I'll pay for it.'

She invariably comes, not when you are sitting alone and rejected, but at those miraculous times when there does happen to be a line of people waiting to buy books. While she talks happily on, I reach round her, trying to sign books for people who are looking at their watches. Somebody's aunt is delighted with me. She has discovered me. She takes up her stand by my table, talking, introducing me, asking people if they have read my book, *I Leap Over the Wall* (by Monica Baldwin), listening to conversation, nodding and moving her lips and repeating the last words of the sentence. Her bus does not leave for hours. She is there for the day.

Then there are the people who come, not to see what an author has written, but because they want you to see what they have written.

A man plunges in with the manuscript of his two hundred thousand word novel, which he wants you to read on the spot. Like the aunt, he never comes when the shop is empty, only when you are lucky enough to have people waiting to meet you. When the man with the manuscript gets going, they often become discouraged and go away.

He wants you to have his novel published, or made into a film, or a television series. He wants you to write his life story.

'My life would make a book. I'll tell it to you. On a tape recorder, if you like, I'm not fussy. You write it, and we'll go fifty-fifty on the profits.'

Some people come out of curiosity to see what you look like, so they can go away and tell their friends that you were nothing special.

'Well then, what was she like?' A husband had waited impatiently at the shop door, while his wife carried out the inspection.

'Nothing extra. I like her jumper.'

Two women in Brisbane watched me from afar. They stalked me round the shelves, spied on me from behind the maps and dictionaries, and stood half hidden by a rack of cook books, peeking at me and giggling. Finally one of them nudged the other forward.

'Did you want to buy a book?' Sometimes you have to ask that, and 'Did you want?' sounds less offensive than 'Do you want?'

'A book?' She was surprised. 'Oh, I don't know. I'm not a great reader.'

Her friend took courage to join her. 'What it was,' she said. 'We were just standing there thinking, that picture of you on the jacket of your book must have been taken years ago.'

When people do buy a book, it is always, 'For my wife', or, 'For my mother who's ill,' in case you might flatter yourself that they want to read it themselves.

When it's a gift, they like you to put the name of the person they are giving it to over your signature.

'She'll be quite pleased. I'm afraid I've never read any of your books, but Ethel is quite a fan of yours.'

In Sydney, a woman came up to me in a department store to buy a copy of my novel 'for a friend'.

'Shall I write someone's name in it?' I asked.

'Emma Chisit.'

I wrote on the title page, 'To Emma Chisit, with best wishes . . .'

'No,' she said impatiently. 'Emma Chisit?'

'Twenty-three shillings.'

When this exchange was reported in the *Sydney Morning Herald*, with the comment that the plural of emma chisit must be hammer charthay, a man called Alistair Morrison realized that the woman in the department store had been talking Strine.

'This incident,' he wrote later in the introduction to his dictionary, *Let Stalk Strine*,* 'made a profoundly disturbing impression on me. I realized that while we all speak Strine fluently and are able to understand each other without much difficulty, there did not seem to be any reliable and comprehensive dic-

* Ure Smith, Sydney, 1965.

tionary of the language available for use by visitors, students, new Strines and people who speak only English.'

Calling himself Afferbeck Lauder (get it?) he offers in his book such Strinery as:

'Miss gem, laze and gem: Usual beginning of a public speech.

Garbler Mince: Within the next half hour. Also Greetings. As in: 'I'll be with you in a garbler mince,' or 'With the garbler mince of the Gem of Directors.'

Gunga Din: Locked out. As in:

A: I gunga din, the door slokt.

B: Hancher gotcher key?

A: Air, buttit spoultered on the inside. I tellyer I gunga din. Car more, nope-nit.'

That's Strine.

18

Although they were getting older, Henry and Fanny still came to us in North Falmouth every summer. Fanny spent more and more time in bed. Henry spent more and more time in an armchair by the fire, or a long chair in the sun, his slipping pince-nez shaded by the battered panama hat that had blown into every Italian lake, the straits of Messina and the river Danube.

Conserving his energies within himself and growing more reflective, he talked to himself a lot, asking the things that he mislaid where they were and who the devil had hidden them. We wanted to put his passports and tickets and travellers' cheques in the safe, but he felt safer with them in a bedroom drawer, although they were always disappearing.

'What's that woman done with my wallet?'

Mrs Catchpole had been succeeded at 52 Chepstow Villas by Mary Vinton, last to inherit the title of 'That Woman', and responsible for all losses, even in the United States.

'What's that woman done with my reading glasses?'

His pince-nez, when they were not falling from a sweating summer nose to smash on the terrace bricks, vanished several times a day.

'Mary Vinton isn't here,' I would have to remind him. 'That woman is me.'

Although we had most meals in the kitchen and the evidence was clear that there were no servants in North Falmouth, he still hoped for lunch and dinner on time. He still would not break his bread on a side plate, but on the tablecloth like a Frenchman, sweeping the crumbs to the floor by way of cleaning up at the end of the meal.

'Henry!'

I shouted at him for tapping the long ash of his cigar deliberately on to the carpet.

'It's all right. They'll take care of it.' He looked round vaguely for dauntless Mary Vinton or her helper gentle Clair Gribben, who were even now scouring out 52, as Minnie Maunder and Mary Lott used to do every August.

'Where are my glasses, Baby?' He had gone back to calling me that, as we both got older. 'What's your mother done with *The Times*?'

When she was in favour, she was Fan, or M'wife. When out of it, she was Your Mother, or an upstairs version of That Woman.

'Where are my glasses, Baby, and what's your mother done with *The Times*?'

I settled him into his favourite armchair and went back to finish in the kitchen. When I turned off the taps, I heard that he was talking, although Fanny and the girls had gone to bed, and Roy was in his work room at the other end of the house.

From the back of the chair, I could see the top of his bald head, permanently scarred from encounters with low beams and doorways in Hinxworth and other English cottages. One hand hung limp over the side of the chair.

'It wasn't my fault,' he was saying. 'It wasn't my fault, you see . . . I wanted to go. I was willing to give my life for my country. But it was my eyes, you see. They wouldn't take me. It wasn't my fault.

Too short-sighted to enlist, he had done wonderful work in the First War, helping the families of soldiers, and rehabilitating men into civilian life when they came back. But fifty years later, this uneasy memory had surfaced from the storage vaults of his mind.

He would rather have gone out to be shot.

How did they do it, the generals and recruiters and propagandists? How did they brainwash thousands of men not only into going out to the mass slaughter of trench warfare, but going *willingly*? Or was the brain-washing self-induced by the treacherous romanticism of those long prosperous years without a war?

At the end of his long life, half asleep in North Falmouth, Henry, who had the luck to stay behind while his brothers went out to be wounded and killed, could still be troubled by the indelible guilt of not being found worthy to join the glorious dead.

My mother-in-law, Grace Stratton, was getting older too. A farmer's daughter from the Middle West, full of grit and energy, she had worked hard most of her life in the anxious battle against bills and rent collectors. Her husband had died when Roy was thirteen.

When he was sixteen, he told his mother he was going for a walk.

'So there was I,' the oft-told story began, 'sitting in my room. I had this terrible cold. He came in and said to me, "Momma," he said, "I'm going for a little walk." I didn't see nor hear from him for three months. Where's that boy of mine? I wondered. It was the Y.M.C.A. told me where he was at the end. "Just going for a little walk," he said. I was in my room. I had this terrible cold. "Momma," he said . . .'

The little walk was a freight-jumping marathon from Richmond, Indiana, to Jacksonville, Florida. He was picked up by the railway police two or three times, but released because he was too young to be locked up. When he was hungry, he played the piano for his supper in bars and restaurants. In Jacksonville, he was sitting on a bench in the sun when he caught the eye of a Chief Petty Officer, although he did not look more than four-teen. In the recruiting office, they said that he was eighteen, and with the sponsorship of a 'guardian' from a neighbouring bar, signed him up as an apprentice seaman.

When snobbish Navy wives in Washington asked me, 'What was your husband's class at the Academy?', it gave me pride and pleasure to be able to say, 'He got to be a commander the hard way.'

They were not as impressed as I was. They would rather he

had done it the easier and more socially acceptable way. Americans like to play at being a classless society, but they can be far more discriminating than the British when they give their minds to it.

The American class structure is at the same time inflexible and marvellously flexible. You can move around from class to class depending on income, job, education, politics and success in sports. While you are in a class, however, you must stick by its rules and labels.

When I first met Gracie Stratton, she was running the ticket booth for a big amusement park on the outskirts of Dayton, Ohio. She lived in a neat little house inside the park grounds. As you lay in the bath by the window, the roller coaster came swooping down every twelve minutes, full of shrieking people, about ten feet away from your naked right shoulder.

It was a good job and she liked it, and liked the excitement and noise of the park, and the bingo games and the memory of the big bands like Glenn Miller and Guy Lombardo, who played 'Deep Purple' and 'When my Dreamboat Comes Home.'

When she retired and came east to be near us, she felt betrayed and lost, and confused by lack of belonging. New England, which seemed so outgoing and friendly to me, was stuffy to Gracie, who had spent all her life among gregarious Mid Westerners who run back and forth borrowing cups of sugar, and drop in on each other constantly, and drive a hundred miles on a Sunday to sit in a hot living room with the blinds half down to 'visit' with the talk that is their sustenance.

'Sit down and visit a spell', is the kindly welcome.

Early in their acquaintance, Henry said to Gracie at breakfast, never his best time, 'Don't you ever stop talking?'

I held my breath, afraid she would not understand that the rudeness of the British is not necessarily intentional.

But she took it as a compliment. 'Me? Gracious, no, I talk all the time,' she said proudly. 'Wonderful, ain't it?'

In North Falmouth, she lived in a little house on the other side of our stable yard, crammed with pictures of Roy and ashtrays in the shape of praying hands and chamber pots that she had picked up in the booths of the amusement park. As she grew older and gave up her job at a local gift shop and her involvement with the church, she was more and more lonely for someone to sit a spell and visit with her.

We were away a lot, so we looked for a companion to live in the house with Gracie and visit and watch television. They would have a nice home, and she would have someone to talk to.

After several weeks, Greta was the only person who showed up for an interview. Anxious about going to London soon, we were so glad to see her that we gave her two manhattans, and the interview went very well.

At first she was lovely. With the television going like a thing possessed, she sat and talked with Gracie by the hour, and went to the shops, and made fancy custards. Whenever she made her delectable little desserts in glasses, she always made four extra for us, and brought them up through the stable yard, and we would give her a sweet manhattan.

Once, after we had been away for a few days, I went down to Gracie's house. The old lady was pottering vaguely about in her kitchen, picking up threads from the rug, rubbing at Greta's cigarette burn on the counter, rinsing out a clean cup, opening and closing the refrigerator door.

'Where's Greta?'

'I don't know, honey.'

'She's gone out?'

'I think she's upstairs. She must be sick, or something. I haven't seen her for a while.'

'How long?'

'A few days ... I don't know.' Gracie had slept downstairs, since she broke her hip.

'Who's been doing the cooking?'

'Oh ...' She looked round vaguely, opened the refrigerator door again, and shut it.

I put some stale bread in the toaster. 'What's wrong with Greta? Have you been up to see?'

'I can't manage the stairs, honey.'

'Did you call the doctor?'

'I can't remember his name.'

'You could have –' I realized that I was bullying her to delay going upstairs. I am not sure what I expected to see. I thought perhaps Greta might be dead.

What I did see, when Gracie was sat down to her toast and cocoa, and I climbed the stairs to the bedroom under the sloping roof, was poor old Greta sitting on an upright chair in the middle of the room, surrounded by smeared glasses and empty wine bottles.

The next companion we managed to find was a dear motherly black woman called Eva. She and Gracie got on very well. They liked the same kind of food, and they liked to sit all day and watch the television, and as Gracie became more dreamy and forgetful, they did not talk very much.

Eva was extremely kind, but Gracie's mind, assisted by a saturation of daytime television, began to lose its grip on reality. She became obsessed by the idea that her companion was in power. Eva was not dominating, nor even opinionated, but Gracie, anxious and confused, began to be afraid.

I would go into the kitchen and find Eva frying chicken, or beating a cake batter in a comfortable, unhurried way.

'How is she?'

'Just fine. She had a good sleep, and she's going to have a nice dinner.'

'Are you happy here?'

'Just fine. Mrs Stratton is a very nice lady.'

I went through into the room where Gracie sat with the blinds down, unperceptively mesmerized by the screen, on which doctors and nurses and bizarrely ill or injured patients played out their endless afternoon dramas.

'How are you?'

'Just terrible. I don't know what I'm going to do.'

When I moved to turn down the television, Gracie said, 'No, turn it up, so she won't hear.'

'Hear what?'

'Listen,' Gracie clutched my sleeve with the blotched, bony hands that had worked so hard to provide for Roy before he went for his little walk. 'I'm afraid,' she whispered urgently. 'She's out to get me.'

'No. She loves you.' I bent to hear what she was saying through the blare of the dark nurse flinging at the blond doctor, 'Hwhen hwill you grant me the respect that is my due?'

'She's cruel to me.'

I was sure this was not true, but since Gracie believed it, it was as bad for her as if it were. When we tried to reassure her of Eva's good will, it only made her imagine that we were on Eva's side in some ghastly plot against her.

Soon after, Gracie became ill and had to go into the hospital. After Eva left, I began to think: But what if it had been true? Not of Eva, who was not capable of even small unkindnesses, but supposing a companion's name was Evil, what a fantastic opportunity to terrorize and control. With replacements impossible to find, the victim's family, willingly hoodwinked because they needed the companion to stay, might have indicated that if she left, a nursing home would be the next step. What a trap of horror for a helpless old lady.

Driving to Boston, I had watched a beautiful yellow house near Plymouth, standing in fields quite close to the road, hidden in summer by thick elms and copper beeches, emerging as the leaves fell to stand exposed beside the noisy highway. On the other side of the road was more grass and some red barn buildings. It was obvious that the new highway had been cut slap through the cow pasture of the yellow house.

It was an ideal setting for a horror story. From an upstairs window in a gable end, I could sometimes imagine that a pale blurred face looked out, captive, mouthing silently for help as the cars rushed by.

One day on an impulse, I turned my car off the road, knocked on the back door of the yellow house, and asked, 'Can I use your house as the setting for a book?'

It was true. The road had been cut through their cow pasture, separating the house from the farm buildings. They had heard rumours about the highway, but not where it was going to be built, until they looked out of the window early one morning and saw men walking through the meadow and driving in stakes.

After the road was finished, a tunnel was made underneath, so that the cows could still go to and from the barn. There were no cows now, and the land where the barn and cowsheds stood was soon to be sold for building. The tunnel, low and sinister, with the thunder of traffic overhead, was used only by the youth of Plymouth for assorted purposes.

There was everything I needed for my story of the old lady and her evil companion. The yellow house had been in the same family since it was built in the early eighteen hundreds by a naturalist who brought trees and shrubs from all over the world to enrich its grasslands. Because he was involved in the back-to-nature movement of the Transcendentalists, his friends were people like Emerson and Thoreau and Louisa May Alcott's father. They were often in this house, whose rooms still looked much the same as in the days of those great idealists.

It was a fascinating place of crooked doorways and creaking stairs and uneven floors and lattices and secret cupboards. If my neighbour in North Falmouth could hear Daniel Webster snoring in her bedroom where he had once lodged when the house was an inn, it was feasible to imagine that a nervous elderly insomniac might hear Ralph Waldo Emerson snoring in the upstairs room of the yellow house by the side of the highway.

The woman of the house was descended from one of those bold few who had survived the terrible first winter in Plymouth, when the Pilgrims lived in the stinking hold of the *Mayflower*, and planted corn over the growing number of graves, so the Indians would not know how many had died. She had planted the herb garden in the reconstructed Plymouth Plantation, and knew everything about the medicinal and kitchen herbs and roots the Pilgrims used in their first village settlement. She taught me about herbal poisonings, which seemed a suitably eldritch choice for the old lady's gruesome companion in the story, which was called *The Room Upstairs*.

19

Although I continued to be Monica who might be met in the greengrocer's to the readers of *Woman's Own*, I was now, after fourteen years across the Atlantic, allowed to write special articles about America.

Not as if I lived there. I could not be Monica who might be met in the drug store or the supermarket. I wrote as if I had been sent over on an assignment to tell the readers about people like Tony Piazza, a fortyish cocktail pianist in Oregon, who had legally adopted two little boys, although he was not married.

In America, as in England, it is still rare for a single woman to be allowed to adopt, and just about impossible for a man. There are not enough 'prime' babies for couples who want them, so Tony, through an enlightened adoption officer, had taken two 'unprime' boys with mixed Spanish and Italian and Mexican blood, abandoned dark-skinned misfits, who belonged in nobody's world and would otherwise have spent their youth in foster care.

I found the three of them in a bright house above Lake Oswego, with pointed fir trees scattered over the rounded green foothills, and the great snowy Cascade Mountains beyond.

'I still had so much,' Tony said, telling me about the loneliness after his divorce. 'I had to share it. Without a child growing up here with me, all I had worked for, everything I had and was – it was worth nothing.'

People do say these good, simple things, and they can go straight into a magazine article without embellishment.

Tony, changing nappies and straining vegetables and rolling about fatly with the boys on the flower-filled grass, seemed far preferable to some of the couples who apply to adopt for the wrong reasons. To patch up a rickety marriage. To be accepted by the local young parents. To replace a lost child.

Calls come from hospitals after a new-born has died. 'My wife wants to take a baby home, so send one along by Friday.'

Tony knew of a couple who had a pony and needed a child to go with it.

After supper, the elder boy fetched him his hair piece as if it were a hat, and he put it on the front of his balding head, tucked his sons up in bed in his own room, and went off down the hill to the restaurant in Portland, where he was 'Mr Piano', a popular night time attraction.

I went to Canada to a village in the forested hills a hundred miles north of Toronto, to see a woman with a brain-damaged child. At fourteen months, Sylvia had gone into convulsions with a temperature of a hundred and eight degrees that destroyed enough brain cells to leave her rigid, spastic, barely conscious, without hearing, sight or movement.

'She'll always be a vegetable,' the doctor told her parents. 'You'll have to put her into an institution and forget there ever was this baby.'

But the mother could not do that. She brought Sylvia home. Her back was arched in a bow. Her forearms were locked upwards, the hands clenched tightly by her shoulders. Her legs were rods, the ankles fixed. Her bloodless face was expressionless. She cried all day and all night. It took two hours to feed her even a small meal, and she vomited most of it back. Her wails and groans were so terrible, and the convulsed sight of her, that even friends who wanted to help could not bear to come. The two older children were neglected, sulky and quarrelsome.

In despair, sleepless and shattered, the mother took her to an institution. In four months, Sylvia lost eighteen pounds. She lay motionless, with flies crawling over her.

'They don't last long,' a nurse told the mother, who picked up the stiff, wasted baby and took her home to die.

She and her husband ran a motel for winter skiers and summer fishermen, and she hung the wasted, dribbling baby in a swing in cabin doorways while she cleaned and made beds. Some visitors were shocked and some too pitying, but the mother did not care. She wanted them to see that by some miracle, the child was alive.

When she was three, she took her to the Institute for Human Potential in Philadelphia, where she learned the principle of patterning. A normal baby progresses neurologically from crawling through creeping on all fours to standing and walking. If the brain cells which convey the messages for these movements are destroyed, patterning attempts to reverse the process. It forces the limbs into a crawling pattern, in the hope that constant repetition will convey the message back to the brain and stimulate unused cells to take over.

Three people had to work on Sylvia's arms and legs and head, twice a day, week after week, month after month. The extraordinary thing about this story is not only that the child did recover some movement, sight, hearing and the beginnings of speech, but that the whole hardbitten mountain village became involved in the patterning. Housewives, shopkeepers, firemen, children, men from the lumber mill and the farms – it was a massive community project that softened taciturn suspicion and healed old feuds.

A few years later, I found the same endeavour at the Air Force base near where we live on Cape Cod. Airmen and their wives, the Base Commander, neighbouring civilians were giving their time to work patiently on the limbs of a puny little boy in the hope that he might learn to walk, or even crawl.

The faith of the mother, like the Canadian woman, was obsessive and consuming. The child and the patterning were her whole life. The only time I saw her weep or despair was when she left. Her husband had been posted to another small base in an unpopulated area. She had had to choose between staying with her child's patterners, or going with her husband and probably having to stop the treatment.

My American publisher suggested that instead of depending

on book sales – only one American in four buys even one book a year – I should do what everybody else was doing: get out on the road and sell myself on the lecture circuit.

Over six months, I gave some sixty lectures in thirty states to a total audience of about thirty-eight thousand – mostly female. I was a part of the fantastic sub-world of women's clubs and luncheon groups and forums and assemblies and conventions and things called Knife and Fork Clubs, which flourish like the fruits of the earth in the fertile Plains states.

On this speaking tour, my engagements fell roughly into two main categories. First there was the proper formal lecture where I stood on a stage in a hall or theatre with a potted plant behind me and rows of women in front of me saying, Go ahead, entertain us. Instruct us. Bring us culture. Make us laugh. Sometimes it was at ten o'clock in the morning.

Some of the women's clubs were enormous. Whole city blocks, and they had their own auditoriums, with a black man to work the lights, who was addressed with nervous bonhomie as Earl or Roger, and looked glum. He would adjust the microphone for me. Cue for tales from the Programme Chairman about Madame Chenault who was there last week, such an itty bitty thing, she had to stand on a box to see over the podium. Miss Dickens, peasant third class, had to have the mike pulled right up, and tilted.

'You should have been here when little Han Suyin came. She was perfectly darling.'

Sometimes I sat on stage while I was being introduced, trying to make my legs look good and watching the trembling flesh of the Chairwoman's calves. What had she got to be nervous about? She didn't have to speak for an hour. But she knew those people. I wouldn't speak for five minutes to people I know.

Sometimes I was left in the wings with Roger, hearing the Chairwoman use my opening joke. In a town in Pennsylvania, once visited by Charles Dickens, who noted only that one waiter had a green glass eye and the other had his fly unbuttoned, I stumbled out at the sound of my name, resplendent in my new white summer suit, and found myself in front of a white movie screen, quite invisible. In Lexington, Kentucky, I gave a racy talk on the homosexual implications of *David Copperfield* from the pulpit of a converted church. An old lady choked in the second row, and I handed her down what I thought was a throat lozenge, but was actually a chlorophyll pill.

The old ladies always sat in the front so that they could hear. After half an hour, the ones who had to go to the ladies' room stumped out, with canes, and then stumped back in again, and everybody turned to look, as if an old lady walking down the aisle was worth far more than what was going on on the platform. Some of the audience, both old and young, fell asleep.

The after lunch and after dinner talks were an even greater ordeal. In an airport coffee shop, I met a history professor who was also on the lecture circuit, and we exchanged notes, like horses conferring together about their riders. He told me that he had instructed his agent to charge fifty dollars extra if he had to sit through a meal, and a hundred if it was creamed chicken and peas with fruit jelly salad and mayonnaise.

The iced water alone would kill you. As in Moline, Illinois, it did actually kill Charles Dickens's fifth child, Francis Jeffrey Dickens, who was a Canadian Mountie. He had crossed the border to Moline to visit a friend on a sweltering hot day, drank a large quantity of iced water and died of paralysis of the heart, which has caused him to be known as the only Dickens who ever died of drinking water.

I almost died of having to make small talk at the head table during the interminable lunches and dinners. If I was staying at the same hotel, I could remember, 'My pills!' halfway through and go upstairs and lie on the bed until I judged it was time to speak. And then come down to sit through a long rambling report from the secretary, votes of thanks to the members who made these darling table centres out of macaroni and wire coat hangers, and Mabel Haffenloder's account of her recent travels in the Greek islands.

By the time my talk was over, the audience was as exhausted

as I was, but there was still the aftermath of ritual conversation before we could escape each other.

There was invariably a woman who came up to say, 'I've come fifty miles' (accusingly, as if that were my fault) 'to tell you that I have a whole set of Dickens's books at home.'

'Never!' I reeled back in amazement.

'I wish my poor father could have heard what you said about Charles Dickens.' She shook her head and nodded it at the same time, so I did not know if she was pleased or angry.

There was a man in a bow tie who knew more about my great-grandfather than I did (not difficult).

'I'm not going to say it was good,' he said to me in Denver. 'I'm going to say it was – er, refreshing.'

And there was always somebody who would rave on about, 'You're really his great-granddaughter! So wunnerful. I was brought up on his works. My family just loves *David Copperfield*. We read *A Christmas Carol* aloud every year, etc., etc.,' and then left me with, 'Well goodbye, Miss Dixon, it certainly was a pleasure.'

20

In 1965, Henry and Fanny came to North Falmouth together for the last time. We had tried to persuade them to fly to Boston, but Fanny had already taken her maiden flight, to Italy that spring, and pronounced it very boring, since there was nothing to see out of the window.

They came by boat, although transatlantic sea travel was not what it had been. One of their favourite small Cunarders was in dry dock, and the feudal barman of the other had at last gone ashore for good. The old liner was shabbier, and so were a lot of the passengers. There were people in First Class who did not change for dinner.

When they got home in September, Fanny was in bed more and more, and finally all the time. People still dropped in to see her on their way home from work. She kept the bottles of gin and vermouth on her washstand, and at six o'clock, Mary Vinton carried the ice bucket up to her bedroom instead of to the drawing room. People still told her their problems, and even when she was feeble, and breathless with emphysema, she still performed the ritual of the 9 a.m. telephone calls to the aunts who were still alive.

'Do you think so? I don't think so at *all*.'

'I never thought her good-looking.'

'What on earth is Monty up to?'

'Come to lunch. We'll have it on a tray up here. Mary Vinton can make *arme Ritter*.'

She still reeled off family doggerel when people were born or married, or when they were ill, although she was worse than anyone.

'Dear Child – it really gets my goat
To hear all this about your throat.
Until tonight have not felt fit
To tell you what I think of it.'

It is fitting that the last poem she ever wrote should have been
to her granddaughter Mary, who is most like her. Mary, who is
my niece and dearest friend, can produce doggerel like Fanny,
but other things as well, and is the writer that Fanny might have
been if she could have had the chance.

The poem is trivial, yet important, because it shows her still,
old and sick, thinking more about other people than about herself. That had always been a genuine instinct of interest, not a
device to get love. And so she got it.

The last time I went to London to see her, when she was very
ill, I took her Mary Clive's *The Day of Reckoning*,* which re-
captures the domestic details of comfortable leisured families at
the beginning of this century. She smiled at familiar paintings
like 'The Doctor', and, 'When Did You Last See Your Father?',
and the germy wicker nursery furniture, and the innocuous Du
Maurier jokes from *Punch*, but I was comforted in a way, to see
that she was not really interested. She was letting go easily,
withdrawing into the private world of her illness, encapsulated
by loving nurses.

She had once said to me, a propos of what I cannot remember,
'Never know your doctor socially', but the young physician who
came every day was more like a concerned son. She had a wonderful Irish day nurse, and at night a tiny chubby Spanish
nun, known as Baby Bundle, who told her not to estarve her
estomach. They sheltered and protected her and cherished her
through the slow concerns of her dying.

I wanted to be there when she died, but you cannot sit about
waiting for someone to die who is not dying to die. They know
what you are up to. Fanny knew what I was up to, and sent me
home. She died on the eve of her ninetieth birthday, two days
after I went back to America.

*Macmillan, 1964.

195

Henry only lived a few months after her death.

They adored each other. They had quarrelled often, and bickered and deliberately misunderstood and wounded, and raked up ancient grievances against each other's parents. But the quarrelling seemed to be a necessary part of the fabric of their marriage bond, and surviving it a triumphant proof of its strength.

Henry's mother was, after all, a Frenchwoman who shouted at the maids, 'You fool!' and bossed and cosseted and nagged at her Harry, until he learned to scold back, 'Marie – tu es idiote!' before retreating again behind the high back and sides of his wing chair.

After Fanny died, Henry used to say, 'We had a perfect marriage.'

I said once, 'But you did fight a lot.'

'Nonsense. Never had a cross word with that woman in m'life.'

For his funeral, Mary Vinton had a wreath made in the shape of his elusive pince-nez – two circles of blue and white violets with a curved bar between. After the ceremony at the graveside, as we turned to leave, I saw her step forward, pick up her spectacle wreath from the pile of flowers and throw it into the open grave with a matter-of-fact gesture that said, as she had often said, 'Here you are then, if you're looking for these.'

Even the foreseen loss of your parents at a normal age brings shocks you have not bargained for. One is that you must finally face the fact that you are grown up. While they are alive, you can be their child, even in middle age. They stand between you and death. With both of them gone, you are next in line.

But that is nothing compared to the unexpected gap, the vast space, not a desert or an emptiness, because a desert has substance, and emptiness implies containment. An infinite nothing.

Fanny seemed to hang about for a few months. There was an unresolved, rather restless sense of her somewhere at the edge of consciousness. Then Doady said to me confidently, 'Well, she's gone.' It took her longer than some people to break free, since she had been so involved with the living.

But a long time after that, I sat in a dream in a chilly, lightless corridor, waiting for my fate to be decided by someone behind a high closed door, chocolate brown, like the dining room door at 52, with a brass knob and hand plate. I groped out a hand to see if anyone was there.

Fanny took my hand. 'Yes, my darling, I am always there.'

I wish that all dreams were as clear and unsymbolic.

It was time to write another book. With each one, I have always said it was the last. Every time I said, 'I'll never write another book,' Roy bought me a new pen, or a more comfortable chair, or built me my desk in the windowed corner, where I can distract myself with the sidewalk life of North Falmouth on one side, and on the other, the garden, with the tree house clinging halfway up the elm, which has formed ringed callouses where the boards rest on its limbs. Beyond, horses graze, or doze head to tail under the maples, or if it is near feed time, gaze thoughtfully at me over the fence.

Perhaps it was the loss of Henry and Fanny that prompted me to go back to the Thirties for the next novel. I thought that it was because the Thirties was the only thing I knew anything about that I had not used in a book, but perhaps it was really a last clutch at slippery adolescence, when one could, in fleeting anger, safely wish one's parents dead, because they were so invulnerably alive.

I sat in the Boston Public Library, reading old magazines and unreeling the Thirties from microfilms of *The Times* to remind myself of what had happened.

Torso found in cloakroom at Brighton station. Legs and arms at King's Cross. Germany withdraws from League of Nations. Outbreak of psittacosis: alarm among parrot owners. Unfrocked Rector of Stiffkey thrown to lions. The King's life is drawing peacefully to its close . . .

Greatest disaster in the history of aviation. The R.101, the biggest airliner in the world, floated forth on its epoch-making flight to India and crashed on a wooded hillside in northern France. All but two of the sixty-two passengers and crewmen died, and with them the future hopes for lighter-than-air flight.

The pictures in the *Illustrated London News* show the saloon of the luxury airship looking like the palm court of a south coast hotel, with wicker furniture and stewards in tail coats. They were shod in rubber, to avoid sparks on the metal decks, since the giant air bag overhead was full of explosive hydrogen, and 'it was the policy of the Air Ministry to take no risks.'

Vast and peaceful, the great silver sausage floated low over the countryside, while passengers in deck chairs looked out of the big windows in the bottom of the hull at frightened cows and upturned faces of the earthbound passing beneath their rubber soles.

After its test flights, the R.101 was pulled out of the hangar at Cardington like a cigar from its case, and towed by airmen to its mooring mast, to the cheers of the crowd and a few cries of 'They'll never get it off the ground.'

But they did. It passed mysteriously over London, where people stared from rooftops, on its way to Ismailia, the first leg of the long risky flight that had been publicized with the new Government slogan of 'Safety First'.

Crossing the French coast, the airship shuddered and rocked through a freak storm. It lost altitude, and the weight of the rain-soaked fabric made it impossible to regain height. At 2 a.m., it went into a steep dive, hit the ground, exploded in a series of blinding flashes and was almost instantly destroyed by fire.

The pictures of that wrecked and smouldering airship look like the twisted skeleton of a downed dinosaur, too ill-adapted to its environment to survive. It lies, half in and half out of the trees on the gentle hillside ten miles south of Beauvais, where Roy and I had once tried to get married after an excellent lunch. Because I had to do all the talking in French while Roy could only nod and grin, the Mayor of Beauvais thought it was a classic case of a G.I. being taken for a ride.

They brought what was left of the victims of the crash home to lie in state in Westminster Hall, although some of the coffins had little more than clods of earth in them, so much had been incinerated. An endless line of sombrely clad people filed over the stone floor to contemplate, not only untimely death, but what seemed then like the death of commercial flying.

After the memorial service in St Paul's, during which a pigeon flew down from the dome like the Holy Ghost, the funeral procession marched to Euston, with Ramsay Macdonald, Stanley Baldwin and Ministers of the Dominions and India walking in slow step behind the horse-drawn Army wagons. Along the railway line to Bedford and the road to Cardington, crowds lined the way like thick hedges. In the twilight of an October afternoon, the flag-shrouded coffins were laid in the mass grave, where relations and dignitaries in morning coats stood with their toes on the stone rim, as if it were the edge of a swimming bath. Three volleys from the firing party. Last Post, then Reveille.

'Tens of thousands of people came pouring over those fields like a sea,' a woman told me in the cemetery at Cardington. She was pottering about with jam jars and wilting flowers, and I pottered with her, while she told me, 'You ought to have been here for the funeral,' like a bookshop manager. 'Tens of thousands. Broke the hedges and trampled through people's gardens. I'd seen it go off, you know. My mother and I had seen it go off and I said to my mother, "It's not raising right." '

I stood with her at the graveside, with my toes on the spot where Stanley Baldwin had planted his sensible round-toed shoes. It is still a haunted place, even after almost fifty years of air crashes that get bigger and more cataclysmic. The national hysteria over the R.101 seems enviably naive now that far more colossal disasters only shake the world gently for twenty-four hours and are forgotten by all except those whose lives they touch.

From the flat Bedfordshire roads, you can see across the fields of market vegetables the huge airship sheds that are used now for experiments with research and weather balloons. In the hangar where the R.101 was welded and stitched together, an old grey barrage balloon sulked under the roof, tied to the floor alongside the gaudy round balloon which was used in *Round the World in Eighty Days.*

The man who showed me round brought out a cigar box

which was the memorial of the doomed airship. A battered cigarette case, blackened coins, a belt buckle, a few buttons. Not much more.

It was raining quite heavily when I drove away between the dripping brussels sprouts, past those neat Bedfordshire houses that surprisingly are made of wood, with chapel-shaped upper windows. I crossed the A1 to take one more look at Hinxworth.

The elms had been cut down on either side of the lane where I used to walk up to May Clements's dairy with my milk can. Hilda's Post Office grocery had been moved to what used to be the policeman's house, next door to the village hall, where I had once led the Women's Institute in Twenty Questions. The workmanlike farmhouse had been painted and modernized, with gardens laid out and Muscovy ducks on a trimly banked pond that used to be a mud puddle.

My cottage, the only apricot-coloured one in the county, had been painted white with black beams, like hundreds of other period cottages in Hertfordshire. The garden looked bigger because the greengage tree had disappeared, and so had the posts that had held swags of Paul's Scarlet and Blaze roses along the path. The cesspool between the garage and the tennis court was rankly overflowing, as it always did when it was raining.

The new kitchen and bedroom I had been building before I left to follow the siren song of the New World, like many a G.I. bride before me, had been sketchily and cheaply finished, although the thatch was good, because there was only one thatcher, and he was good. The rosemary bushes by the door, the hollyhocks, the jasmine, the cotoneaster, the lavender, the cooking apple tree – I still felt they were mine. The house reproached me. I did not go inside. The owner, who was a pig farmer, was out farming pigs.

I walked on past Fred and Hilda's bungalow, where my goat shed stables seemed to have reverted to goat sheds, but the middle one still had the Rose and Crown sign the children hung out for their pub, which had brought the licensing authorities round to see what was going on. I turned down the green lane that was the start of so many rides. Hoofprints of other horses and ponies paddled the sucking mud between the dikes that bordered the barley fields. For a moment, I wished that I had stayed. There would never be hedges and bushes like this where I knew every twig, never those firm turfy spots under the tree with the roots like the arms of a chair, where you could sit and smell cow parsley and look at Ashwell steeple.

Illusion. The dangerous moment passed. What exchange was any of this for the human love and companionship and stimulating conflict of the life I had now? If I had stayed in Hinxworth and kept everything just as it was, I would have been the fifty-year-old aunt of all those children now grown up and gone away and grumbling at letters that said, 'You ought to go and see poor old Mont. She was good to you when you were young.'

The novel that I wrote round the crash of the R.101 was about a young woman in love with a murderer, sharing his life in hiding, dragged down by his brutality, but unable to be free.

Looking back on myself in her period of the early Thirties, I began to see that it was more than just an impulse for adventure that had sent me into other people's kitchens for two years as a cook-general. It had also been an attempt to dispose of insecurity by shoving it under the rug of new and engrossing experience.

Memory brought that out and looked at it. I saw how fat I had been, how awkward, how inconveniently dependent on outside opinion. Bold and vain sometimes in a new dress and hair do, I could feel instantly a mess when that inevitable cool red-head came smoothly into the room to spoil my evening. Dragging out the hurts from under the rug of *One Pair of Hands*, I found a new repository for them in the clumsy, boyish girl in *The Landlord's Daughter*, who was in love with a murderer.

I gave her the pimples that spoiled country house weekends by poking shinily through the heaviest make up if you did not squeeze them, and flaming into the threat of blood poisoning if you did. The weekends themselves, which you had to accept,

201

because you were a failure if you stayed a weekend in London, unless it was for a special party or a special man.

With young men I met on the debutante circuit, and at Oxford and Cambridge with my friends' brothers, I went to house parties for hunt balls in the Shires, and coming out balls in Hampshire, although I did not like house parties, balls, or even those particular men.

I got out of trains at wayside halts miles from anywhere, when there was no one to meet me, and it took an hour before the village taxi driver finished his tea and came to drive me five miles to the chill manor house, where other people's M.G.s and Baby Austins were parked on the gravelled drive, and everyone seemed to have paired off before I got there.

You allowed almost anyone to kiss you, rather than return home unkissed, or without having your buttons undone and breathing heavily to show you were feeling what you were supposed to be feeling. With not much talk about it, either publicly or privately, you were not quite sure what everyone else was doing. When girls lost their virginity, it was often because they were too gauche to know how not to without losing face, which might be worse.

21

All my writing life I have known that a book is not a book until it is read. There must be a reader as well as a writer to complete the mysterious process of creation.

Pictures in the writer's mind and the emotions he feels are transformed through his arm and hand into black marks on white paper. The marks, which mean nothing in themselves, are then converted by the eye of the reader into pictures in his own mind and a stimulus for his emotions. Very much the same emotions and pictures, if the black marks are in the right arrangement, although each person's interpretation of the same book is slightly different.

A manuscript that lies unread in a bottom drawer is not yet a book. To make possible the mysterious cooperation between writer and reader, they must be introduced to each other. The publisher is the essential go-between.

Ever since he said to me in the Paddington Baths, 'You ought to write a book about it,' Charles Pick has been essential to me with support and love, and the nourishment of the faltering ego which is necessary if one is to go on doing something as egotistic as offering books for people to buy and read. Without the luck to have a publisher like this, I don't know that I would have continued to write, however many pens and chairs Roy bought me.

Fanny said, 'Never know your doctor socially,' which I interpreted wrongly as regret over a long-ago indiscretion with our family doctor, whose prawn eyebrows emerged from the mists of chloroform after he had taken out my tonsils on the kitchen table. But 'Never know your publisher socially' – that would be a sad loss, and if your publisher is one of your best friends, you have had my kind of luck.

Charles said at lunch, hoping I was not stuck in the Thirties for good, 'If you're thinking about the next novel –'

'I'm not.'

'When you're thinking about the next novel, why don't you look for some good strong – sort of social theme?'

'Like what?'

I was in my usual foggy limbo between books, with nothing in my head at all, and anything I could ever know or imagine already written, too many times.

'Well, you know . . . a life and death thing. I'm not sure what I mean. Probably not something like The Samaritans, but –'

I don't remember any more that was said, because I stopped listening.

The Samaritans is a world-wide fellowship of men and women of all ages, creeds and races, dedicated to befriending people who are desperate enough to want to kill themselves.

If people want to kill themselves, why can't they?

They can. But then why don't they just go ahead and do it, instead of ringing The Samaritans for one last chance?

I went to the Samaritan centre in London to talk about the isolated and lonely people who I knew must be among their callers. I was thinking of someone in a big office where people know the names only of people in their own department, and very little more about them than their name. I was thinking of someone called Mildred, who types all day, or does invoices or checks figures, and is a very proper and discreet person who wears neat knitted suits, polyester in the summer, and is assumed to be all right, because she never looks or sounds as if she were not.

At five, she puts the cover on her typewriter and goes home, but nobody knows where she goes or what it is like, and when she is unexpectedly out of the office for two or three days – 'Not like her not to let us know' – and is found hanging behind the door, or on the floor with an empty bottle of pills, everyone says, 'I can't understand it. We never knew there was anything wrong.'

Chad Varah, who founded The Samaritans in 1953, is an extraordinary person, very hard to describe. The only all-purpose word that can be used is idiosyncratic.

The recruiting slogan The Samaritans have developed to convey their need for quiet, unpretentious volunteers who do not know all the answers is, 'Are you ordinary enough to be a Samaritan?' Chad is not ordinary at all. An ordinary person could not have recognized and organized this method of befriending which is so simple, so direct, and so purely human that it can work anywhere in the world.

The original London centre is in the crypt of a City church called St Stephen, Walbrook, behind the Mansion House. I sat in one of the little furnished cells made in the old burial place for people who come to talk or weep or just sit quietly. We talked about Mildred going back to her flat, where she never has a visitor and never invites a visitor, and three day weekends are a nightmare, and about young people staring at the wall in college dormitory rooms while people assume, if they think about them, that they are studying.

At The Samaritans, I began to realize for the first time how common to every human being is the potential for suicide, given a certain situation and a certain state of mind. I began to see how many people do walk this perilous knife edge between life and death at some time in their lives. It is perhaps the possibility of suicide in all of us that makes people afraid of it and unwilling to talk about it. If Mildred, instead of putting the cover on her typewriter and going home, were to say, 'I can't go on any more,' Alice at the next desk does not ask, 'Have you been thinking about suicide?' She is more likely to say, 'Isn't life hell? I know just how you feel. Cheer up, dear, soon be Friday.'

What secret was it that The Samaritans had discovered that could help to save lives that might be lost in a crisis of despair? How had they managed to spread their unassuming network all over the United Kingdom?

'The only thing I've done,' Chad said, 'is to make it possible for the right kind of people to be instantly available to those who desperately need someone to talk to.'

'Would I be that right kind of person?' I was forgetting about Mildred and her typewriter cover.

'You can try.'

In 1953 when Chad, concerned about the rising number of suicides, decided to start a one man telephone service in his City church, he thought that since the exchange would be MANsion House, a suitable number would be MAN 9000. St Stephen, Walbrook, had been bombed in the war. Picking his way through the wrecked vestry, he found a telephone under some beams and rubble. He lifted the receiver. It was still working. He rang the business office and asked that whoever else had MANsion House 9000 should be persuaded in any way possible to give it up.

'We can't promise anything,' was the answer. 'What number are you calling from?'

He brushed chalk dust off the front of the dial. The number was already MAN 9000.

People came to the church seeking help and also offering help. The offerers listened to the seekers. Recognizing the value of these ordinary listeners, Chad stepped back and let them answer the telephone.

There are now five or six lines in this London centre. When I started to work there in 1968, there was only one emergency telephone. It sat on a desk, black and old fashioned and to me filled with menace. Even after going through the preparation course, I knew that if I picked up the telephone and somebody said, 'I'm going to kill myself,' I would not be able to cope.

The telephone rang. I looked round for someone to answer it. A lot of people had come in to talk, and most of the volunteers were busy. One of them said, without turning round, 'Somebody answer that.' I picked it up.

'I'm going to kill myself.'

For the first time in my life, I knew what it meant to be 'at a loss'. I had lost everything. I not only did not know what to say. I physically could not say anything. My mind had gone away and left a hole. I actually saw blackness.

'I'm going to kill myself,' the very young voice repeated patiently.

I managed to ask why.

'Because I'm pregnant and I can't tell my parents.'

All I had to say was, 'But you can tell me,' but I could not say it. I did not even think of it. I stammered something inappropriate and she hung up.

I ran up the steps out of the crypt to the Underground station. *How dare you?* My mind was not empty now. There was a voice sounding in it like a gong. How dare you, with your pretence of concern for people, with your Mildred and her typewriter and your dabbling in human misery to make into books that don't even approach reality? How *dare* you have been the one who picked up the telephone at that particular moment in this girl's life? She will kill herself, and you will have to kill yourself too, because you will never forget it.

Halfway down the escalator, feet came behind me. The man who had said, 'Somebody answer that' grabbed my arm. He did not say anything, but when we got to the bottom, he turned me round and we went up again, out of the station and back to the centre.

The befriending the Samaritans do is not reserved for the people who turn to them for help. They befriend each other, in order that they can go on befriending. The uncritical reassurance I got from the volunteers was my first experience of feeling accepted as myself, without having to woo, or pretend, or cover up.

But I rightly did have to pay for my arrogance in assuming that wanting to be a Samaritan made me a suitable person to be one. For nights and nights after that, all the weeks I was in England, I lay awake thumping my shoulders into the pillow, with the short, intensely awful conversation playing over and over again in my head, like the sound track of a bad film.

'I'm going to kill myself.'

Gasp. Silence.

'I'm going to kill myself.'

'Why?'

'Because I'm pregnant and I can't tell my parents.'

'Why – I mean, are you sure –'

The irrevocable click as she rang off and the uncaring dial tone.

Even after I found out that she had rung back the same afternoon and talked to somebody else, I remained obsessed, tortured by guilt, sick with disappointment. The two voices, her desperate one and my own stupid one followed me wherever I went. Once on the escalator coming up from Piccadilly Circus station, anxiety seized me in a strangling grip. I could hardly breathe. There was a pain round my chest, a crushing iron band. I thought I was having a heart attack. A man was standing in front of me with a briefcase. I said, 'Oh, please,' but not enough sound came out. I put out my hand to touch him, but he stepped up out of reach.

At the top, I managed to get into a taxi, and I went home and sat in a chair and held myself tightly, as if I were a vase that had been shattered into a thousand cracks and would fly apart if I let go.

The anxiety attack had the same physical symptoms as a broken heart. Once, on a visit to America after the war, I had fallen in love, found out the man was married, and jumped on the next boat to take my wounds home. A broken heart feels exactly that – physically broken. The first two days of the trip, I sat bent over as if I had had an abdominal operation, with my arms wrapped round myself to hold what was left together.

How to get rid of the voices? I went back to North Falmouth and wrote about them. That has always worked for me. Having got rid of the guilt, you then have to deal with feeling guilty about not feeling guilty. Guilt is the most pernicious of all the emotions. Also the most useless. It does not help the wronged person, and it can destroy the one who feels it. If guilt could be eradicated from the repertoire of human emotions, there would be fewer suicides.

The novel about The Samaritans was called *The Listeners.* In America it was called *The End of the Line*, because Taylor Caldwell had stolen *The Listeners* before I even thought of it.

With most books, you are intimately involved while you are doing the research and the writing, but as soon as the book is done, you seem to have written it out of your system, and are ready to become absorbed in something else. But two years after I wrote *The Listeners*, I was still working with The Samaritans every time we went to London.

Why had nobody ever started a Samaritan branch in the United States? Americans were too professionally minded, I was told. You could never run a volunteer service on as little money as they do in England. Nobody would give you any money anyway. Psychiatrists would hate you because they would think you were trying to steal their customers. Nobody would volunteer. Furthermore, nobody would ring up.

I thought I would have a go. As I went round Boston finding out who would help, one person led me to another, and each time I banged the pillow with my shoulders at night, in terror that I had taken on something bigger than I could handle, somebody turned up who was just what I needed.

A doctor who understood about befriending. A journalist who wrote an enthusiastic article. Someone with some money. Someone who could type. The right kind of volunteer, recognizable anywhere in the world, an ordinary person who can shut up and listen.

Would anybody contact us? You must evaluate community need for this service modality, bureaucrats told me. If you have any funds, you must spend them on a task force survey to determine if there is an experiential Felt Need.

It seemed quicker and cheaper to advertise a telephone number and see if anybody rang.

In the first four years of the Boston branch, there were more than two hundred thousand calls and visits. Other branches have started in Massachusetts and other States.

My life has changed. I had thought that writing was enough, but it is too egocentric a way of life to be honourable.

What do The Samaritans do? Mostly they listen.

'I've got to talk to somebody.'
'I'm here. Please talk to me.'
'I can't go on like this any more.'
'Like what? What's wrong?'
'Everything. I can't stand it any longer.'
'Tell me about it.'
'I can't. It's too awful.'
'Is it so bad that you're thinking about killing yourself?'
'Well . . . yes. Yes, I am. But I've never told anybody. I don't know why I'm telling you. Do you trace calls?'
'No, of course not. You're perfectly safe. Tell me what's wrong.'
'Everything. This man and I – well, we've been together for about a year. And well . . . I'm going to lose him. He doesn't know that I know. I guessed he was seeing his wife again, but he's too much of a coward – no, that's not fair, he's not a coward, but he's trying to make it easier for me, I suppose. Well . . . I'll make it easy for them.'
'By killing yourself.'
'Yes.'
'Have you thought what you'd do?'
'I've got pills. Enough.'
'Have you taken anything? Do you need medical help?'
'I took one. One or two. I'm all right. I'm afraid though.'
'It's all right. Don't be afraid. I'm with you.'
'Is it all right if I – I mean, I'm so alone. I can't stand it. I've got to talk to somebody.'
'I'm so glad you rang us. We'll talk for as long as you want.'

'Samaritans, can I help you?'
'Yes. I want to know, if a person took ten valium and some aspirin, what would that do?'
'It would depend. Can you tell me why you need to know?'
'Well, there's this woman I know. She's got some pills, and I'm afraid she's going to take them.'
'Does she want to die?'

'I don't know. She's very mixed up. She doesn't know what she wants. She's done it before – taken pills, I mean. Someone found her.'

'Was she glad?'

'I don't know. I don't know how she felt. I told you, she's very mixed up.'

'Are we talking about you?'

'Yes.'

'Can you tell me what's wrong?'

'I want to make sure I do it right. My therapist told me if I overdosed again, he'd put me back in the hospital. I couldn't stand that. I'd rather be dead.'

'Who is that?'

'This is Steven. Can I help you?'

'Where's Heather?'

'I'm afraid she's not here tonight. Could you –'

'I've got to speak to Heather. Get her for me.'

'I don't think I can do that. Please talk to me. Perhaps I can help.'

'I don't want to speak to a man. Who are you anyway? Are you a priest? A psychiatrist of some sort?'

'No.'

'What's the point then?'

'Do you want to talk to a priest or a doctor?'

'I don't want to talk to anyone like that. That's why I rang you.'

'I'm glad you did.'

'Why are you glad? People don't like talking to me. I make them angry. You'll be angry.'

'Try me.'

'This is Jimmy. I don't know what to do. I walked out of school, but I can't go home. My Mum would kill me.'

'Did something happen at school?'

'It always happens. I'm always in trouble. And it's worse at home. Everybody hates me.'

'It must be awful to feel like that.'

'I wish I was dead.'

'Oh Jimmy ... it's all right. I'll wait. Don't worry. Crying's all right. I'm here. I'll wait till you can talk.'

What do The Samaritans do? Nothing spectacular, like talking people down off bridges and twelfth storey window ledges. We are hoping to reach people before the final crisis, before suicidal thoughts have to be translated into action. Suicide prevention seems an ugly, too forceful expression, and yet prevention is the right word, in the same sense as preventive medicine.

Desperate people do have choices. Suicide is one of them. Ringing The Samaritans is another.

22

Ever since I was eleven years old, I have had horses. It started when Chilworthy was sold and Fanny bought the cottage in Oxfordshire with an American girl called Biddy, whose family were friends of ours. It is not finished yet. I still keep horses in North Falmouth, and hope to go on keeping them even after I have to be hoisted into the saddle with a block and tackle, and can do no more than potter down the road and back before tea.

Horses process extraordinary amounts of expensive food through one end and out at the other, and unless you are winning prizes or selling horses or manure, there is no material profit.

Roy used to comment on that when the feed bills came in, although he knew, because I had taught him to ride, what the real profits were. But in the end I did find a way to turn to some account all the horses I have ever had in my life. I started to write children's books about horses for the passionate reproductions of the little girl that I had been, refusing to wash the smell of horse off my hands, and crying into the soup at Sunday supper.

It was an indulgence, but sanctioned. My sister Doady, who was a school librarian at the time in a district of south London where about niney per cent of the children had probably never touched a horse, much less sat on one, had said, 'I can't satisfy their hunger for horse books. There are never any left on the shelves (Oh, Miss Dickens, your books are always on our shelves). You've spent most of your life with horses. Why don't you write about them?'

'All right.' It was one of those instantly recognizable ideas.

'And while you're at it,' she added, 'write a series. If the libraries buy the first book, then they have to go on and buy the others.'

When we first started to spend weekends in the white cottage by the duckpond in Britwell Salome at the foot of the Chiltern Hills, wearing corduroy riding breeches that bagged between waist and knee like plus fours, my first pony was called Chips. She came from Dartmoor and had a triangular chip snipped out of her ear, by way of a brand.

Every Friday afternoon, Majer the chauffeur came to the school in the blue Wolseley car whose celluloid windows let up and down on straps like a railway carriage, with Nanny Gathergood and enough sardine sandwiches for us and the friends who came with us. Every Sunday afternoon, Majer turned up again in Britwell, and I had to put away the baggy breeches in the bedroom that looked out to where the chalk road went straight up Britwell hill to the clump of beeches on the skyline, between fields of short, tough turf dented by my pony's hoofs.

Chilworthy had been a magical microcosm of fantasy and small freedom within the larger world of the grown-ups' making. In Britwell, the whole world was ours, created by children for children. Biddy lived in the cottage all the time with cats and dogs and chickens and ducks and two nocturnal bush-babies in the apple attic. She was in her twenties, and although she sometimes seemed grown up if we got out of line about something serious, like the horses, most of the time she was a child, devising a child's way of life whose adventure and pleasures were limitless.

It actually did have some limitations, of the horses' schedule, times of the Norfolk flavoured meals that Nanny cooked, and the boundaries of the weekend, but it felt like total freedom.

When I started to write children's books, I instinctively tried to recreate this impression of a world without the restrictions of grown-ups. Without thinking about it, I devised a situation where the parents were out of the picture most of the time, and the children were living on their own with animals. I thought this was because I had been irritated by the presence of parents

in children's books who were either too repressive or too understanding, always brutally saying No, or giving gentle homilies
in the first person plural: 'When we grab everything for ourselves, we end up with nothing', but I see now that it was a
subconscious attempt to recreate what to us was a world made
for children in Britwell,

The cottage was comfortably primitive, the rooms small, with
brick tiles downstairs and creaky, uneven boards upstairs, and
everything going on in the kitchen, where bridles hung on door
knobs and you had to move a saddle off a chair before you
could sit down.

Instead of plumbing, there was a groaning rain water pump
in the scullery, tin baths before the fire, and an earth closet down
a path outside the back door, overgrown with wet privet. You
tipped in a shovelful of earth and ashes when you were finished,
and old Calcott from the village grumbled away with the bucket
somewhere up the garden twice a week.

In winter, we went to bed in jerseys and socks, and there were
coal fires in the narrow bedroom grates. In summer, we took the
iron beds to pieces, and put them up again in rows on the lawn.
Even Nanny, brought up quite primly, learned not to mind
when Calcott, coming early to work, found her in nightdress
and slumber net beneath dew-beaded blankets and a furious
morning chorus of birds.

When it was hot, we rode across the fields to the river tow-
path near Benson, and Biddy drove Nanny and the picnic in the
two-wheeled trap behind Gemma, mother of Tonia, who kicked
the governess cart to pieces fourteen years later. I had a short-
tailed pony called Jenny, bought out of a butcher's cart in
Wallingford, who would plunge into the river and wallow and
roll. Just as she was getting up, I stepped on to her bare back,
and she swam with me in the muddy water.

When it was raining, we bought chocolate toffees from the
tiny shop in the side wall of the Red Lion, and played Mah
Jongg interminably, like bridge addicts in the smoking room of
a cruise ship.

Biddy did have a snub-nosed Morris car with a dickey at the

back, but we went all the shorter journeys by horse power. Riding late on autumn nights, with a certain damp sharpness to the air, the furred edges of the horse's ears glow with phosphorescence. Home-going shod hoofs strike sparks from the flint road. The stable yard is streaked with yellow shafts of light from the lantern hanging above the straw. Ethel May Gathergood has baked apples with treacle and crusty suet, exploding as the fork goes through in a cloud of hot mush where the boiling jam is hidden.

Nothing changes. When I lived at Hinxworth, I tried to re-create this same kind of world for Doady's children. There were always ponies and horses. Hal wore a riding hat in bed. Pip cleaned his saddle in the dining room. Mary fell off at a standstill and broke her arm, just as Doady had done in Oxfordshire when she forgot to tighten the girths. We went to horse shows, and covered the landscape on long rides, galloping on the Royston downs and finding a broken stretch of that green Saxon road called the Icknield Way, along which years before Jenny and I had raced the little train that ran between Watlington and Princes Risborough.

In North Falmouth, there have always been ponies and horses. When we first came here in 1953 with Pam, I thought that now I would be a wife and mother and settle down. We had not been here two weeks before a woman came leading a chestnut horse down the drive. She said that he was wild, and I could have him if I liked. He was only wild because she used to beat him up. We built a stable and fenced in some land and bought another horse, and ponies as the girls got older.

There were always five girls here in all the holidays. Roy's son married three months after we did. Their three children are the nieces of my daughters, but close in age, like cousins. For the third time in my life, it was horse shows, long rides on the beaches and the sandy trails through the scrub oaks of Cape Cod, village gymkhanas in our field, bridles on door knobs, someone watching television in pyjamas and a riding hat, always children round the kitchen table, endlessly, obsessively talking about horses.

What is it about horses that keeps me still so involved that I would make all sorts of sacrifices to be able to keep them with me? Just going out to the stable to feed them in the morning is a fresh pleasure that never becomes a task. I stand beside them while they eat, and breathe in the heady scents of their skin and breath and the malty smell of the feed. I walk out at night to listen to them moving mysteriously about the fields, tearing at the grass in the unceasing effort to get enough roughage through those twenty-two yards of digestive tract.

In 1962, driving to a film studio to write a script for a film of *The Heart of London* that was never made, I used to stop and visit the Home of Rest for Horses, which was then at Elstree. There were about sixty horses, some fit, some groggy, some rescued from ill-treatment, some sent there to live out their dotage in earned peace. I could not help writing about it. It was the book about cruelty to animals, that made my cousin protest at the party that I ought to be writing about cruelty to children.

My English sporting friends were shocked.

'Did you see what she wrote about hunting? I think she's gone mad.'

'We stood up for you,' the kindest told me. 'We said you were having the change of life.'

The publishers accepted it calmly, but hoped that I had now got horses off my chest. But ten years later, thanks to a horse-mad actor called James Bolam, it was picked up by Yorkshire Television and made into a children's series called 'Follyfoot'.

They rented a tumbledown farmhouse and outbuildings near Harewood, pulled down bits of it and built them up again to look tumbledown in a more picturesque way. Here they acted out the horse dramas, and my oldest granddaughter spent two summer holidays working in the stable, doubling in distant riding shots for the main characters, and seething because the director could not understand that if the child on the screen rode into the farm yard and tied her pony up by the reins, every horsey little girl in the country would be worrying too much about whether it would pull back and break the reins to be able to follow the rest of the scene.

Since 'Follyfoot' was shown all over the world, wherever there are horsey little girls, which is everywhere, I was allowed to write another book called *Talking of Horses*, into which I put everything I ever knew or guessed about them. I suppose I have got it off my chest at last, although I still spend hours in the stable, or leaning over the gate of the field where the horses tear at the grass in their unceasing effort to get enough roughage.

23

I did not write another grown-up book for several years, although I had characters waiting. For some time there had been a quiet young man with soft brown hair hanging about at the edge of my mind. He was wearing a white jacket and I thought he was a nurse. I made him a private nurse, so that he could be picaresque, in a novel called *Last Year When I was Young*, which was also a repository for one of those chunks of poetry which inhabit the mind for years, comfortably, but inhibiting new entries, like old regulars in the best chairs of seaside hotels.

I had finally got rid of Alfred Noyes's 'The Highwayman', which I had programmed into myself at age twelve when I memorized any poem that had a horse in it, by using 'the landlord's black-eyed daughter' in the book about the murderer and the R.101.

The mild young man in the white jacket with a watch and scissors in the pocket took over Belloc's verse:

> 'From quiet homes and first beginning,
> Out to the undiscovered ends,
> There's nothing worth the wear of winning,
> But laughter and the love of friends.'

I have not got rid of it, even so. The last line still dominates. I want it to.

Why is this so hard to write about? Why is it so difficult to write about friendship that I have left it until the end of this book?

It was not casually that Belloc linked laughter and friends as the richest prize on the journey to the undiscovered ends, and not by chance that I recognized his truth. Certain things, read for the first time, leap from the page as so familiar that you could almost swear you had written them yourself – only someone else has done it better. I have needed friends for companionship, reassurance, solace and to ward off the fear of having somehow to manage alone. But oh, I have needed them for laughter more than anything, and it is the laughter that I remember when I look back at the treasured cast of true friends who have come and gone, or are still with me.

When I was a small child, I kept a list of people I was in love with. Nobody I knew. There would have been no magic in that. I loved, among others, the Prince of Wales, a soldier with his arm in a sling in a play called *Alf's Button*, Saint George in *Where the Rainbow Ends*, one of the lost boys in *Peter Pan*, and one or two members of the Surrey County cricket team.

Henry, who took me to their matches at the Oval as if I were a son, could have introduced me to the cricketers, but that was not the point. The list was the point, a possession, a talisman. I had all those names under my pillow. I must be all right.

Later, the unwritten list of real friends became the talisman.

It was not until I listened to the desperately lonely people who contact The Samaritans that I began to understand what friendship is, by seeing how terrible and damaging it is to try to live without it.

The knowledge of even only one, not very close, friend provides some sense of belonging. If you do not belong anywhere, it is hard to survive. One of the common elements in suicide is the pain of loss, and the final loss is the conviction that there is no place at all where you safely belong. You are worth nothing, even to yourself. Especially to yourself. There becomes no point in not killing yourself.

People are able to survive for years in a deadly marriage or a dull job, because they do at least belong there. The crippling routine of housework, a production line, a viewless office with anaemic plants – even Mildred's desk and typewriter cover may be what has kept her going all these years. Simone Weil once said that what keeps people committed to a cause is not so much the cause itself, as being part of the way of life among those who serve the cause.

Along with the accompanying chorus of laughter, friends have played different parts with me in different acts of life.

In early childhood, they were the sharers of secrets and fantasies, a miniature gang, even of only two people, against the hazards and unpredictability of the larger world. Older and less vulnerable, in the years of Norland Place School and the cottage in Oxfordshire, the company of friends doubled the pleasures and dramas. I also learned that if you had friends available, you could safely discover the positive joys of being on your own.

Alone, I began to be aware of the individuality and essences of animals and growing things, and what their living had to do with mine. Weather was no longer just something that dictated whether you played out or indoors, and whether my brother would sprawl grumbling on the sofa. I became conscious of the effects of sun, wind and rain on my physical self and sought them eagerly, influenced by the sky. Fantasies were no longer shared, and became more powerful and exciting.

It was safe to explore solitude when the friends were there to go back to. Joan, Barbara, Sylvia, Audrey, Pat – if they did not ride ponies, I forced them to. We lay awake with firelight on the ceiling in the cottage bedrooms, a serious seminar of giggling.

Older still and more insecure, friendships were more competitive. I picked a few loyal dodos whom I could dominate, as well as the girls who were more attractive and sophisticated than I was. To some of those I was the loyal dodo. To the closer ones, I was all right to be seen out with, but just far enough behind not to be a threat.

St Paul's was given meaning and colour by my friendship with Ann, who had long beautiful hair and later betrayed me by getting engaged to my brother before I was ready to believe we were grown up. In Paris there was the other Ann, who taught me to be reckless, in that house in Passy where Madame chased

Yvonne with the meat cleaver – or was it Yvonne who chased Madame? – and we were locked in our rooms at night.

In a brief aberration at the Central School of Speech Training and Dramatic Art, tyrannized over by wonderful, petrifying Miss Elsie Fogerty, there was Maimie. Since we had both chosen the wrong profession, the laughter was even more necessary.

The Central School was in the Albert Hall in those days, with kidney-shaped classrooms round the circular walls where, bulging awkwardly in black tights, I mimed fear, joy, anger, doubt, maternity and leading a reluctant dog. I recited glorious, heroic poetry with gentle Miss Brown, who was transformed by it, and stumbled through the maid's part in a rotten play we had to do because it had enough parts for women. For a ritual mass penance, we had to go on to the stage in the vast auditorium and recite a sonnet, while Elsie Fogerty sat in the farthest box and shouted, 'I can't hear you, my child!'

'When I consider how my life is spent . . .'

I recited 'Milton on his Blindness'. Maimie recited 'If I should die, think only this of me . . .'

Elsie Fogerty told Fanny that I had bow legs – what did she expect after eight years of horses? – and they would have to be broken and reset. Fanny, covering her nervous anxiety with the small dignified poise she was able to summon at times of crisis, said, 'We'll wait and see.' Good thing she did, because shortly after that, I was thrown out of the acting school for not being able to act.

I had made such a fuss about being allowed to go there – 'Why couldn't I go on the stage? You never give me a chance, etc., etc.' – that I had not the nerve to admit defeat. I still went off every day on the 52 bus with my tights and play scripts and poetry books, and wandered about or went to the cinema until it was the right time to go home.

One afternoon, Henry, walking home early, found me reading on a bench in Kensington Gardens.

'Why aren't you at the school?'

'I was expelled.' I looked at his shoes, the turn-ups of his striped trousers, the brass tip of his umbrella.

'Why didn't you tell us?'

'Well . . . I thought you'd be angry.' Not fair. It was because I felt like an idiot. 'You've paid for the whole term.'

'Angry? I'm delighted. We only let you go because we hoped it wouldn't last long.'

We walked home together.

The friendships of the war in factory and hospitals were of that intense, lifeboat variety – we're in this together. The laughter was triggered by shared esoterica, and although we had needed each other desperately, most of the friendships lasted not much longer than the circumstances which created them.

With the permanent, lifetime friends who age with you and are till death, there is no need to be in each other's pockets all the time, as there was when you were younger. Even if you meet only rarely, each knows that the other is there.

These are the friends I cannot write about, for some reason, any more than I can describe what I feel about my husband and my children. How define one's life blood?

Index